AFRICAN LANGUAGES POETRY ANTHOLOGY:
VOL 1

Edited by Tendai Rinos Mwanaka

Mwanaka Media and Publishing Pvt Ltd,
Chitungwiza Zimbabwe
*
Creativity, Wisdom and Beauty

Publisher: *Mmap*
Mwanaka Media and Publishing Pvt Ltd
24 Svosve Road, Zengeza 1
Chitungwiza Zimbabwe
mwanaka@yahoo.com
mwanaka13@gmail.com
www.africanbookscollective.com/publishers/mwanaka-media-and-publishing
https://facebook.com/MwanakaMediaAndPublishing/

Distributed in and outside N. America by African Books Collective
orders@africanbookscollective.com
www.africanbookscollective.com

ISBN: 978-1-77928-410-5
EAN: 9781779284105

© Tendai Rinos Mwanaka 2025

All rights reserved.
No part of this book may be reproduced or transmitted in any form or by any means, mechanical or electronic, including photocopying and recording, or be stored in any information storage or retrieval system, without written permission from the publisher

DISCLAIMER
All views expressed in this publication are those of the author and do not necessarily reflect the views of *Mmap*.

About editor

Tendai Rinos Mwanaka is a multidisciplinary artist, writer, musician, editor, publisher and producer with over 70 individual books and curated anthologies published in US, Northern Ireland, UK, Cameroon and Zimbabwe. He has 5 music albums, with new album, *For Mberikwazvo: The Winter After* (2025) recently released and his music is playing in at least 18 radio stations in US, Canada, UK, France, Israel, Brazil and Australia. He has hundreds of paintings and drawings, thousands of photographs, some exhibited, published and sold. His pieces have appeared in over 500 journals in over 35 countries and his books and writing is translated into at least 11 languages. His music can be licensed here: https://www.songtradr.com/tendai.mwanaka. And find him here: https://m.facebook.com/tendai.mwanaka

CONTENTS

Sithembele Isaac Xhegwana (South Africa): Poems in isiXhosa
UMZOBO KAMHLEKAZI U HINTSA, AH! ZANZOLO
HINTSA'S PORTRAIT
IMIBUZO NGEE MEKO ZEMVELAPHI
QUESTIONS OF IDENTITY
AMASIKO NOBUNGCALI BAKWANTU
RITES OF PASSAGE
UMTSHAKAZI OTHINJIWEYO
THE CAPTURED MAIDEN
UMTHWALI WAMAQANDA ENCINIBA WASE KALAHARI
OSTRICH EGG CARRIER OF THE KALAHARI
Abigail Vanessa Bwakila (Tanzania): Poems in Kiswahili
BARUA YA MAPENZI KWA MWANAMKE
A LOVE LETTER TO A WOMAN
KUCHUKUA HISA
STOCK TAKING
WAKATI EPIFANIA INAPOKUJA
WHEN AN EPIPHANY CAME
15 AUGUSTI 2021
15TH AUGUST 2021
MTI WA ASUBUHI
MOTHER TREE
Aliker p'Ocitti (Uganda): Poems in Acholi (Luo)
Kec Opoko Kin Gweno Ki Okwata
How Famine Brought a Rift between the Hen and Eagle
Kwoo Pa Okwata
The Eagle's Vengeance
Lam Pa Min Gweno
The Hen's Curse

Oscar Gwiriri (Zimbabwe): Poems in chiShona
Nyarara
Be Calm
Ngavararame zvavo
Let them live
Kuchema nakuchema
Mourning after mourning
Rudo rweDandemutande
Online Affairs
Kudetemba
Poetry
Ndinodei?
What do I want?
Aisha Hussaina Idris Manarakis (Nigeria): Poems in Nupe
WUN A FE KPANDARA ZAKANMA
THE BRIDGE OF MORTALITY FOR MANY
NYIZAGI NA E JINBO BAGI NA
A WOMAN WITH AN ACT OF A MAN
YETU YI DANBO
THERE'S STILL HOPE
EFO YIZHELE
A DAY TO LIVE...
EGWAFIN YA YEGBOROLO
UNITY FOR PROGRESS
Mujaheed Matashi (Nigeria): Poems in Hausa
Ma'askin Dare
The Midnight Barber
Gindin Magani
The Root of the Cure
Souad Zakarani (Morocco): Poems in Arabic
ح ى النن ام

So we don't sleep
ابتهاج
Joy
كن حرًا
Feel Free
وأنتَتغادر
While leaving
Oladele Babajamu (Nigeria): Poem in Yoruba
ÀSẸ̀ OGUN KORÒ
WAR IS A BITTER DISH
Wafula Khisa (Kenya): Poems in Lubukusu (a dialect of Luhya language)
Basecha Bano
These Men
Nanjala Wange
Nanjala My Love
Sumba Kienyuma
Wretched Men
Jabulani Mzinyathi (Zimbabwe): Poems in chiShona)
Ndosvoda
Ashamed
Afrika
Africa
Zvedu
Inheritance
Dzidziso Dzavo
Their Teachings
Mapfupa Achamuka
Bones Will Rise
Jalaludeen Ibrahim (Nigeria): Poems in Hausa

A DAREN YAU
TONIGHT
SARAUNIYA KYAKKYAWA
MELANIN QUEEN
Bonface Nyamweya (Kenya): Poem in Ekegusii
Ekeng'entambori
The Forget Me Not
Mthulisi Ndlovu (Zimbabwe): Poem in isiNdebele
UKULUNGA LOKUQONDISWA
Ngcali Angelica Xhegwana (South Africa): Poems in isiXhosa
Iimvakalelo
Senses
Inqugwala elingcwele
The sacred old hut
David Chasumba (Zimbabwe): Poems in chiShona
Handina kuvinga sadza pamusha pano
I did not come for Sadza at this Homestead
Regai ndinyarare hangu
My lips will be sealed
Ndipembedzewo mudzimai wangu
Compliment me, my love
Mhodzi yamakadyara: Rangariro
The Seeds That Bore Fruit (in memorium)
Maramba Doro
Binge Drinking Blues
Ousmane Sanogo (Ivory Coast) : Poems in Bambara
Kouma naani (quatre parole)
Foyi téyi (il n'y a pas de problème)
Miri (Pense)
Poyi kê (faire la poésie)
Usman Danjuma Osu (Nigeria): Poems in Iloyi (Ejiri/Afo)

LOH PWAH KWOYAH MI
GRANT MY REQUEST
YIMOH-RIMAH ALUGBAGA
ARISE, YOUTH TODAY
Baxton Chipeta (Malawi): Poems in ChiChewa
NKHANZA ZA CHILENGEDWE
CRUELTY OF NATURE
NDINALI POMPO
I WAS THERE
CHIFUKWA CHIYANI
BUT WHY
ABWANA
THE GREEDY MANAGER
Iwuagwu Ikechukwu (Nigeria): Poems in Igbo
ANYỊ NILE BỤ OBERE CHI
WE TOO ARE GODS
NNE BU IHE
MOTHER IS THE LIGHT
Ismail Bala (Nigeria): Poems in Hausa
Yawon Duniya
The Voyage
Haruffai Shida
The Six Letters
Barin Zuma
A Sweet Lick
Yanci
Freedom
Gwagwarmayar Kauna
The Love Battle
Masaka Madeda (Kenya): Poems in Kidawida
Icho Chai Chiao?
Where is this Tea?

Mwai wa Kidawida
The Beautiful One from Taita
Marina gha Kidawida
Kidawida Names
Wei ni Wacheambai
That they're not from Around Here
Chumbo ra Kidawida
Kidawida Songs
Obuchere James (Kenya): Poems in Luhya
OMWANA OMUSHE NIYAMEELA.
WHEN THE LAST BORN IS A DRUNKARD
MWIKULU
HEAVEN
OMUHEELWA WANJE
MY BELOVED.
Rogers Lobeleng Sethole (South Africa): Poems in Sepedi
MPHE NAKO!
GIVE ME A CHANCE!
MOŠOMO WO
THIS LABOUR
MOENG KA GEŠO
A VISITOR AT MY HOMESTEAD
LE HLANKELA MANG?
WHO ARE YOU SERVING?
Simbarashe Andrew Kashiri (Zimbabwe): Poems in chiShona
Mwari tirangarireiwo
God remember us
Inini ndaikuda …
Personally, I loved you …

Abdullatif Eberhard Khalid (Uganda): Poems in Gikuyu and Kiswahili
THIINI WA GÛTÛRÛRÛ
THE BEACH
MALAIKA DHIDI YA SHETANI
ANGEL VS DEMON
Viti vitupu—
Empty chairs remain—
Jeshi Bila Wanajeshi
Army Without Soldiers
WEWE!
YOU!
William Khalipwina Mpina (Malawi): Poems in chiChewa
Sindili Chimodzimodzi
I am Not the Same
Thambo la Mvula Likadza
When the Rain Cloud Comes
Ifésinàchi Nwàdiké (Nigeria): Poems in Igbo
Haiku Anọ Maka Nnem
Four Haikus for Dear Mother
Haiku Ano Maka Nwam
Four Haikus for Dear Son
Vihje Ben Nkhunga (Malawi): Poem in chiChewa
IMFA YA MAYI
MAMA'S DEMISE
Saratu Muhammad Adamu (Nigeria): Poems in Hausa
KEWAR MASOYI
LONGING
MACE
WOMAN
Yawo Baba (Togo): Poems in Ewe
DZUDZƆUƆNUDƆDRƆ

STOP JUDGING
ƉUTIFAFA ƑEAMEDƆDƆWO
PEACE AMBASSADORS
NYAWO ƑEAKUNYAWƆWƆ
THE MAGIC OF WORDS
AƑENƆ SI TSIAKOGO LA
THE LONELY
Bala Abubakar Daddere (Nigeria): Poems in Hausa
Rayuwa
Life
Rabo
Fortune
Bakuwar Tilas
The Inevitable Stranger
Mai Hasada
The Envious
Gaskiya Dokin Karfe
Truth, the Iron Horse
Aryan Kaganof (South Africa): Poems in Afrikaans
Is die esel 'n donkie?
Is the ass a donkey?
Ek is onsigbaar sonder whisky
I'm invisible without whisky

CONTRIBUTOR'S BIO NOTES

Sithembele Isaac Xhegwana is a multi-award winning South African poet. During 2024 he won the most prestigious South African Literary Award in the poetry category. He was born on the 22nd of May 1972 at Grey Hospital in King William's town. He is qualified with a BSocSc (HONS) in sociology from the University of Cape Town and also a Master of Arts degree in Creative Writing from the same university. Through funding from the NRF SARChI Chair of Critical Studies in Sexualities and Reproduction, he is presently registered for a PhD degree in sociology at Rhodes University. He is presently working as a curator for Amazwi South African Museum of Literature. He is also serving as a member of the National English Language Body for the Pan South African Language Board. At different occasions he has served as an English selector for the national Department of Sports, Arts Culture publishing hub. He has also served as an adjudicator for the English Academy of Southern Africa Sol Plaatjie translation award. His debut novel, *The Faint-Hearted Man* was published by Buchu Books in 1991 and was longlisted for the Noma Award for publishing in Africa. His entry, *Loneliness* was shortlisted for the 1991 Maskew Miller Longman Young Africa Award. He has published 3 books through Mwanaka Media and Publishing: *Dark Lines of History* that won him South African Literary Award for poetry, *Iziyaca*, and *Ntombentle*

My name is **Abigail Vanessa Bwakila**. I am a twenty-nine year old Tanzanian poetess. I am at my happiest when I am composing a poem. I communicate through my poems and it is the only way I know how to. My poems come from the inner workings of my soul and that is where they have always resided. Reading my poems gives you a peek into my wayward mind; they present you with a glimpse of who I am as a person and how my mind works. I hope you enjoy reading them as much as I enjoyed their creation.

Aliker p'Ocitti is a Ugandan Published Poet, Author of a Memoir *(My Mayor. The Political Campaign Story of a Poor Elite and Rich Illiterate); Hidden Scars*, a poetic compilation and also Co-Authored, *Unsaid Words*. His poems have appeared in *Tampered Press, African Global Networks (AGN), Musings During a Time of Pandemic: A World Anthology of Poems on COVID-19, I Can't Breathe: A Poetic Anthology of Fresh Air* and the *Best "New" African Poets 2020*. Aliker is also the founder of Author Aliker Foundation and Author Aliker Publishers that focuses on training creative writing to teenagers and publishing their works.

Oscar Gwiriri is a Zimbabwean published in more than 65 books, both fiction and text books. His two books *Hatiponi* and *Chitima nditakure* were NAMA awards nominees in 2019. He is a Certified Forensic Investigations Professional (CFIP) and a Certified Information Systems Security Professional (CISSP). He also holds a Master of Science in Strategic Management Degree, Bachelor of Business Administration, Associates of Arts in Business Administration, Diploma in Logistics and Transport (CILT, UK), Diploma in Workplace Safety and Health, Commanding United Nations Peacekeeping Operations Certificate, and many other professional qualifications. He likes writing in his vernacular language (Shona) most. His latest Shona book, *Nhemeramutupo* (2025) appeared from Mwanaka Media and Publishing.

Aisha Hussaina Idris Manarakis hails from Bida Local Government Area of Niger State. Born to the family of Alhaji Idris Muhammad Bida (N'One) and Hajiya Sa'adatu Yannagi. She studied Mass Communication at Fati Lami Abubakar Institute for Legal and Administrative Studies (FLAILAS), Minna, and is currently a Ibrahim Badamasi Babangida University, Lapai student. She is a Nupe Writer, Teacher, Translator, Newscaster, Presenter, working with Badeggi 90.1 Fm, LapaiTv and a member of Minna Literary Society (MLS).The vibrant Hussaina is the Vice President of Nupe Writers Association of Nigeria and the Chairperson Nupe Female Promoters Forum, the Coordinator of Millennium Africa Global Initiative (MAGI), Bida chapter. Hussaina, from her teenage days has been in promotion of Nupe language. She is the author of many books in Nupe language which include; 'Bicicin kpako', 'Kangari', 'Ewo na Soko kin na', 'Yetu egi' among others. She has featured in several anthologies of Nupe books. Her work was also published in *Tulu (A Multilingual Anthology of Northern Nigerian New Writings)*. She has unpublished books; Children guide, Nupe poems e.t.c.

Mujaheed Matashi is a bilingual poet from Kano, Nigeria, who writes in both Hausa and English. He has co-published two poetry collections and in 2025, he emerged third place in Leadership Newspaper's Short Story Competition. His works explore mysticism, memory, and indigenous wisdom.

Mujaheed also leads Ruhin Adabi, a collective of writers passionate about cultural expression and poetic craft.

SOUAD ZAKARANI is a Casablanca-based poet, Translator & Writer. Her first publication by BRENTANO GESELLSCHAFT was quite the experience that improved her writing process. She writes in Four Languages, capturing the beauty of fleeting moments with gentle contemplation. She is currently working on her first poem collection «ROSENTROPFEN". She develops a style that aims to blend traditional form aesthetics with contemporary sensibilities, always striving to find the extraordinary in the ordinary. Anthologies in Austria, Germany & Spain: *"Im Fadenkreuz der Archetypen: Märchen, Sex und Gender"* (Quest by Wiener Verlag) https://amzn.eu/d/4t2lowg

Oladele Babajamu is a fellow of the National Defence College of Nigeria and a fellow of the Association of Nigerian Authors [ANA]. He retired from the Nigerian Army in the Rank of Colonel in 2011. He served as Missile troop commander in OPERATION LIBERTY in Liberia in 1990. He was a former PRO [N] of ANA National and two terms Chairman of the Kwara State Chapter. His oeuvre includes, *From Grass to Greatness* [2020] and *War is a Soured Dish* [2023] amongst others. His poems have appeared in various anthologies such as ANA Review and Five Hundred Nigeria Poets amongst others. He is a recipient of the Nigerian Army Chief of Army staff Commendation Award in 2005 for his consistent literary contributions to the Nigerian military. Col Babajamu is a part time lecturer at the Thomas Adewumi University Oko, Kwara State.

Wafula Khisa is a Kenyan poet, writer and teacher. His poetry and prose have appeared in various (Online and in print) literary journals, magazines and anthologies such as *Nthanda Review, The African Writer Magazine, Tuck Magazine, Elixir Magazine, Scarlet Leaf Review, Writers Space Africa, The Legendary Magazine, Dwarts Literary Journal, Agape Review, African Voices: Call for Freedom Poetry Anthology, Nalubaale Review Literary Magazine, Armageddon & Other Stories, Lunaris Review (issue 7), Advaitam Speaks Literary Magazine, Aubade Magazine, Antarctica Journal, New Ink Review, Local Train Magazine, Hope- An Anthology of Poetry, Better Than Starbucks Poetry & Fiction Journal and Best 'New' African Poets Anthology series* among others. His poetry has also been translated into French. He was longlisted for the Babishai Niwe Poetry Prize in 2018. He has published two collections of poetry: *A Cock's Seduction Song & Other Poems (2019)* and *When I Hear My Mother's Voice & Other Poems (2022)* and a short story collection: *Nearly Every Man is Mad? and Other Stories (2022)*. He has also co-edited a short story collection: *Beyond the Pulpit & Other Stories (2024)*.

Jabulani Mzinyathi is a writer born in Zimbabwe. He writes in both English and his mother tongue. He has had several poetry collections published. He has also had a chiShona novel published. It is entitled Mumambure. He has in his closet several unpublished poems. Having read books like Decolonising The Mind and Moving The Centre by the late Professor Ngugi wa Thiong'o, Jabulani is seriously contemplating writing predominantly in chiShona, his mother tongue. Jabulani, like his compatriot Dambudzo Marechera reads with self-punishing acidity. Look forward to more from this imploding explosion.

Jalaludeen Ibrahim is an education specialist, creative writer, and lecturer currently with Federal University Birnin-kebbi. He earned his PhD in English Linguistics from the prestigious University of Bergen, Norway; a Master's degree in English from the esteemed University of Manchester, the United Kingdom; and a Bachelor's degree in English from the renowned Usmanu Danfodiyo University Sokoto, Nigeria. Jalaludeen, the pioneer Coordinator of Kebbi Hill-top Creative Arts Foundation, is the author of *Beyond the Setting Sun* (novella) and *Trance* (poetry volume). He co-edited *Echoes of Carnage* (a collection of poems on Zamfara). His poems, reviews, essays, book chapters, and short stories can be found in local and international outlets.

Bonface Nyamweya is a Kenyan poet and novelist. He is a PhD in Philosophy candidate at the Catholic University of Eastern Africa and teaches philosophy at Chuka University.

Mthulisi Ndlovu, also known as KingKG or KhuluGatsheni, is an award-winning Zimbabwean poet, academic writer and cultural activist born in Plumtree and raised in Bulawayo. He writes in several languages including isiNdebele, English, TjiKalanga, Shona, Zulu and German and is best known for his globally acclaimed epic poem *UBUNTU (The Raw Truth Unravelled)*—the longest poetic work on Ubuntu ever published. He is the founder of Ubuntu Afro-Publishers & media, and the philanthropic trust TROVOCO, dedicated to uplifting marginalized and underprivileged children. Ndlovu has authored and co-authored multiple academic and nonacademic publications and continues to champion indigenous literature and cultural preservation across Africa and beyond.

Ngcali Angelica Xhegwana was born on the 25th of November 2007 at St Dominics Private Hospital in East London. She is presently doing her Grade 12 at Byletts High School at Mooiplas, East London. Her first book, *Woodland* was published by Unicorn Press in 2018. Her second book, *Udyakalash'onkone* was published through the Via Afrika WPR program in 2019. Under the auspices of the National Research Foundation Intellectualisation of African Languages Chairmanship and Via Afrika, her book was one of the twelve titles that was identified that year. *Land Of Thorns*, a book in which she has collaborated with her father, is her third book. During 2020 she was one of the commissioned poets towards the 2020 AVBOB poetry anthology, *I Wish I Had Said... Vol. 4.*

David Chasumba (snr) is a Zimbabwean Writer and Poet. He has published two short story collections with Carnelian Heart Publishing: 2023 NAMA award winning, *The Mad Man on First Street and Other Short Stories (2022)* and *Behind the Façade and Other Stories (2024)*. David's poems have been published by Kalahari Review, Ipikai Poetry Journal, British Haiku Society anthology (2023), in *Best "New" African Poets (2023)* anthology and in *MEN: An International Anthology of African and Latin American Writers, Volume 3* and in *Zimbolicious 9 anthology*. David lives in Bexhill-on-Sea, East Sussex, UK.

Ousmane Sanogo est un étudiant en Philosophie à l'Université Allassane Ouattara de Bouaké (Côte d'Ivoire), c'est un jeune poète-écrivain qui a participé à plusieurs ouvrages collectifs dont Best New African Poets Anthology (2020) et Un voyage dans les vies : douce découverte de la poésie de Jordan Goulet.

Mr **Usman Danjuma Osu** is a poet of Nasarawa state origin, Nigeria, West Africa; a Senior Lecturer teaching English Language, Literature and Creative writing; this he has done in many institutions of learning, and now in the Federal Polytechnic Nasarawa, Nasarawa State, Nigeria. He speaks "Iloyi (Ejiri/Afo)" through which his entry here reflect, as one of the major languages spoken in his state – Nasarawa State, Nigeria where his both parents were indigenes till their Denise at good old age, leaving him a senior orphan today.

My name is **Baxton Chipeta** and I am 21 years old. Currently, I am staying in Kasungu. I am a fourth year student at Lilongwe University of Agriculture and Natural Resources (LUANAR). I am pursuing a Bachelor's degree in Communication and Journalism. Writing has been part of me since I started embracing reading. Whenever I look at this world and whatever we are passing through as individuals, I always have that nudge to write up something. I am a creative writer, having written so many short stories by now. I am also a poet having written lots of poems and some published in Weekend Nation Newspaper. When I got this chance of trying to embrace our local language, I was like why not? So I gave it a shot.

Iwuagwu Ikechukwu is an African poet, dramatist, screenwriter, translator and essayist, a native of Umunkwo in Isiala Mbano, Imo State, Nigeria. His poems, short stories, reviews and essays have appeared in literary magazine across the world. He enjoys solitude, teaching, researching, or reading the works of Christopher Okigbo, Isidore Diala, Chimamanda Adichie, Buchi Emecheta, Ifesinachi Nwadike. He can be reached on facebook @: Ikechukwu Iwuagwu.

Ismail Bala writes in English and Hausa. His poetry and translations have appeared in the UK, the USA, Canada, India and South Africa, in journals such as *Poetry Review, Ambit, New Coin, Ake Review, Lunaris, A Review of International English Literature* and *Aura Literary Arts Review*, among many others. Born and educated to university level in Kano, he did his post-graduate studies at Oxford. His poems have been translated into Latvian, Belarusian, Nepalese, Slovenian and Polish. He is a Fellow of the International Writing Programme of the University of Iowa. He is the author of *Line of Sight* (Praxis, 2020), *A Span of Something* (INKspired, 2024) and *Ivory Night* (KSR, 2024).

Obuchere James was born and bred in Kakamega county, western kenya. He is a poet, an essayist, and a short story writer. He attended the local Eshinutsa primary school and Mwihila boys high school where his literary journey was launched. He was inspired by the likes of Prof Chinua Achebe, Ngugi wa Thiong'o, Grace Ogot, and other literary luminaries from Africa and beyond. To date he has contributed to various anthologies [poetry, short stories and magazines]. Some of his poetry collection form part of Kenya's junior secondary schools study material.

Rogers Lobeleng Sethole was born on the 11th of January in Sebayeng, a small township situated north-east of Polokwane city. He attended the following schools and university: Dithabaneng Primary School, Maphuto Primary School, Mafolofolo High School and University of Limpopo. Rogers is a professional educator whereby he is teaching Sepedi Home Language and English First Additional Language. The author co-wrote a Poetry book titled, 'MAMAPO A TŠA SEMANA'; he was featured in Sepedi Short stories anthology titled, 'RE ALOŠITŠE'; and lastly, his poem were included in a multilingual poetry anthology titled, '100 ECHOES OF MADIBA'S CENTUARY'.

Simbarashe Andrew Kashiri discovered his love of poetry at age 13 when he noted the reactions from his elementary classmates when one of his earlier poems was read out loud to the class. Since then he has published several poems in the now defunct, Gweru based, Moto Magazine from the age of 16. He has also had his Shona poems read out on air on Radio 2 – now Radio Zimbabwe around 2000. Since then he managed to publish a full length poetry book in 2005 with Publish America in the United States of America. He went on to win a medal and 5 Editors Choice Awards with the International Library of Poetry in the 2010s. He has also published poems in several other poetry publications and is a regular contributor to BNAP- Best New African Poets. Academically, Mr Kashiri holds a B.Com (Hons) in Accounting, a Professional Diploma in HIV/AIDS Management and Counseling. He also holds various other qualifications and certifications in various disciplines. He lives in the Midlands Province Gweru and he's married with 4 kids. He writes poetry whenever he's inspired, and feels that there's something he needs to let out

Abdullatif Eberhard Khalid (The Sacred Poet) is a Ugandan passionate award-winning poet, Author, educator, writer, word crosser, scriptwriter, essayist, content creator, storyteller, orator, mentor, public speaker, gender-based violence activist, hip-hop rapper, creative writing coach, editor, and a spoken word artist. He offers creative writing services and performs on projects focused on brand/ campaign awareness, luncheons, corporate dinners, date nights, product launches, advocacy events, and concerts, he is the founder of The Sacred Poetry Firm, which helps young creatives develop their talents and skills. He is the author of Confessions of a Sinner, Vol. 1, A Session in Therapy, and Confessions of a Sinner, Vol. 2. His poems have been featured in several poetry publications, anthologies, blogs, journals, and magazines. He is the editor of Whispering Verses, Kirabo Writes magazine issue 1 and edits at Poetica Africa.

William Khalipwina Mpina is a distinguished Malawian literary figure, celebrated for his contributions to poetry and literature. He co-edited "Walking the Battlefield" (2020), a bilingual anthology of poems reflecting on the Covid-19 pandemic, and authored "Mooning the Morning" (2022), published by Montfort Media. Additionally, he wrote "Kamwala Kodabwitsa" (2024) as part of the Invisible Child Project, funded by Pen International. His most recent work is a short story collection, "Stranger in Her Own Skin" (2025), published by Mwanaka Media and Publishing. Mpina holds significant roles as Treasurer General of the Malawi Union of Academic and Nonfiction Authors and as a member of the Executive Committee of Pen Malawi, a local chapter of Pen International.

Ifésinàchi Nwàdiké holds a Masters in English from the University of Ibadan, Nigeria. His debut collection, *How Morning Remembers the Night* was First Runner Up to the Association of Nigerian Authors Poetry Prize, 2020 and was Longlisted for the Inaugural Pan African Writers Association Poetry Prize 2022. A 2018 Ebedi International Writers Residency Fellow, some of his works have appeared in Maroko, Nokoko, Brittle Paper, Kalahari Review, Olongo Africa, BookArt Ville, Lunaris Review, IHRAM Press, and elsewhere. He is currently a Fellow of the Black Orpheus Exploration Fellowship. He is the Founder and Chief Editor of Ngiga Review.

Saratu Muhammad Adamu is a young writer and poet from Kano, Nigeria. She is 23 and a graduate of BSc. Ed. Chemistry from Northwest University Kano. Her passion for reading and writing has been a significant source of inspiration, and she has written several poems that reflect her thoughts and experiences. She is always excited to share her work with others and explore the world of readers. With a strong desire to grow as a writer, she always welcomes new opportunities and challenges that will enhance her craft.

Vihje ben Nkhunga - an avid reader, writer and ardent poet. A member of Malawi Writers Union (MAWU), Poetry Association of Malawi (PAM) and PEN international (Malawi Chapter).Published in anthologies and local newspapers. Ghost written several prose and poetry works. Edited several short stories that won local prizes, edited Tiseke and the Tree(a children's book by Aubrey Chinguwo). Established Writer's

Club at Nanthomba Community Day Secondary school. A practicing medical practitioner, but a great literally enthusiast.

Born in 1986, **Layeni Okweti or Fyakr Menth'or Baba (Yawo Baba's pen_name)** is a multi-disciplinary artist, philosopher, teacher, culturalpromoter and togolese social activist. Handworker and passionate of arts,culture and environment, Layeni is used to working on several west african subregion projects.

Bala Abubakar Daddere is a poet from Nigeria. He is the immediate past chairman, Association of Nigerian Authors (ANA) Nasarawa State chapter. He works with Nigerian Independent Electoral Commission; INEC as an election administrator. He is currently a Doctoral student in the English and Literary Studies Department of Federal University of Lafia, Nigeria researching in Ritual Poetry. He is the author of a collection of poems titled Tidal Waves, 2023.

Masaka Madeda is a writer, and a teacher. He has written two poetry anthologies, Diwani ya Wasaragambo and I Came to Gather Rosebuds. He is also an active Scout leader and conservationist at Chanikiwiti Scouts Group

Aryan Kaganof is editor and curator of the South African cultural journal herri (https://herri.org.za/10/). His poems have been published in New Contrast, New Coin and Stanzas.

Introduction

After running the Best New African Poets for 10 years we decided to unbundle it and refocus it for the next 10 years. We broke it into 3 anthologies. The first one will revert back to the original BNAP 2015, where we only accepted 3 poems written in English, French and Portuguese, now in its 11th year, entitled *Best New African Poets 2025 Anthology*. The second one now known as *African Chapbooks Poetry Anthology, Vol 1*, already under print, collects at least 10 African poets' Chapbooks into one anthology in English, French and Portuguese. And the third one is *African Languages Poetry Anthology Vol 1*, which is this anthology whereby we give space to our African languages, thus we only take poetry written in African languages. Here when we say African languages we mean languages created by Africans in Africa.

This anthology has poetry from every region of the continent, poets writing and living in South Africa, Zimbabwe, Botswana, Tanzania, Uganda, Kenya, Nigeria, Togo, Ivory Coast, Morocco and Malawi. We have poems in 21 African languages: chiShona, chiChewa, isiXhosa, Sepedi, Afrikaans, Arabic, Yoruba, Igbo, Hausa, Nupe, Ewe, Bambara, Kiswahili, Gikuyu, Ekegusii, Kidawida, Lubukusu (Luhya dialect), Olushisa (Luhya dialect), Acholi (Luo dialect), isiNdebele, and Iloyi (Ejiri/Afo). Languages that predominates are Hausa, chiShona and chiChewa

Poets worked from their traditions and cultures to craft poems that deal with an array of human issues, from identity, culture, traditions, love, relationships, death, spirituality..., and the poems through translation into English still retained their essence: rich language, rich traditions and powerful thoughts that have guided each culture through the ages.

Sithembele Isaac Xhegwana (South Africa): Poems in isiXhosa

UMZOBO KAMHLEKAZI U HINTSA, AH! ZANZOLO

Kwimiqingqo-mizobo yase Ngilane umile.
Egutyungelwe zii ntetha ezi mbaxa
zengcinezelo yamaNgesi, usamile,
yena elutshaba olunganikezeliyo
lokukhula kwe ngcinezelo yamaNgesi –
imbali ye Mfazwe yobuzwe.

Ukubiwa komhlaba ngobuchule bezandla
benkulungwane yeshumi elinesithoba
yobuthanda Ndalo bamaNgilane – ilizwe
elibiweyo.

Apha umile, njenge sithunzi sobukuMkani
bamaXhosa. Ekwathi ngenxa yokukhula
kobu rhalarhume nenkqatho yee-politiki,
u Njengele u Smith owaba ngumthengisi
wobuKumkani nelizwe wamgebenga
kokungenalusini.

Kodwa, lo mzobo awusoze ukwazi
ukubhentsisa iimvakalelo zamazwi
amaninzi asakhalela isihlalo
sobuKumkani esabiwayo, vutho
ndaba lwayo lwaba kukutshiswa
kobuhlanti buka Mhlekazi uHintsa
nokudlavuzwa komzimba wakhe.

Okona ku khwankqisayo kwaba kuku
dinjazwa kwentloko ka Kumkani
kuba gqali naba seki bemeko
yengcinezelo yamaNgesi.

HINTSA'S PORTRAIT

Through English picturesque, here
he stands. Overburdened with colonial
lexicon, he still stands, an intransigent
opponent of colonial advance –
narrative of the war.

Possession of land through
nighnteenth century Romantic
imagination – ceded territory.

Here he stands, as a figure
of Xhosa Royality. That only
through political maneuvering,
Smith could be the true meaning
of a traitor.

Yet, this portrait cannot reflect
the realities of the many voices
still crying for a ceded throne,
Of which the climax was
the burning of Hintsa's kraal
and the mutilation of his body.

And even more, the exportation

of the king's head to the colonial masters.

IMIBUZO NGEE MEKO ZEMVELAPHI

Ezantsi kwam, umnweba owambese
ilali engumzobo omhle, imi okwama-
chaphaza aqingqiweyo, ihonjiswe
zii ntili ezindilisekileyo. Lo mnweba,
ufuna ukuzinza kwii nduli apho mna,
ndifana noswele ilizwi lokuthetha,
ndinqwenela ukuhluba umvandedwa
wam kuzo.

Ebunzulwini bezi nduli, mna,
sele ndilufincile uhambo
olugqunywe zezinye iinduli
eziphakamileyo, nduli ezo
zenza amathandabuzo
ukogqitha obu buhle bendalo
buvuselela iimvakalelo zobutyala
ngaphantsi kwee nyawo zam,
ndiziva ndikhubazekile , ngaphaya
kokhubazeko olubonakalayo
ngamehlo,

ukuzakuza ngalembonakalo
yendalo icikizekileyo. Ndizibone
zizika, lama nqugwala engca,
nezindlu ezithwele ii qhiya
zama cangci akhazimlayo.
Ndikhutywe yhile mbonakalo,

ndizibona ngathi ndigwencela

kweyona ntaba iphakamileyo.
Ndindedwa, ndingcangcazela,
ndifumana ubunzima ekuqapheleni
oovulindlela. Ndikhuphele konke,
kwii mfihlakalo zezi nduli zingama
lolo – ndinethemba lokuba akukho

ne mpunde eyakuze izazi ii mfihlo
zam ezinzima – ndiyehla ndizokwanga
ihlazo lam elandileyo: kuyo lendawo,
eyaziwa nguMoya ongaphezu konke,
ndenze isigqibo sokuyiqamba njenge
lona khaya. Akuncedakali nokuba

zibukhali kangakanani ii mpikiswano
oku kuzibona ndihamba ze, kungoku –
kanye ngoku qha – apho ndikhanyiselwayo,
ngokona bukhali bugqwesileyo, ukuba
okwenzekileyo, kwenzekile –

okugqithileyo kunga kungathi kuya
ginywa ziziseko zexesha elimileyo.
Ngapha koko, mhlawumbi kunokwenzeka
ukuba ubukho bam apha buphehlelelwe
zezinye ii meko, hayi ezi zinga zinobango
olunzulu kum.

QUESTIONS OF IDENTITY

Below me, a picturesque
valley, dotted, with undulating
hills. This valley, wanting to nestle
on the hills that I, dumbfounded,
wish to confide in.

Deep in these hills, I,
having rounded other heights,
more abstract than the guilt-inducing
panorama below my feet, I sense
inabilities, far beyond those of sight,

in defining this scenery. I saw
them sink, these grass thatched
domes, these corrugated iron
roofs. Upon the swift impact of this
view, I seem to trudge to an even higher

peak. Alone, shivering, I struggle
to locate any pathfinders.
Having confided all, in the secrecy
of these desolate hills – trusting
that no one would ever hear

my dark secrets – I walk down
to face more of my humiliation:
in this place, that only a higher
force knows why, I have decided
to call home. No matter how

sharp the contradictions that this
vulnerability confronts me with,
it is now – and only now –
that I absorb, with an even
sharper precision,
that what has been, has been –

the past almost shuts out
in the present. And even more,
that perhaps my presence
here is for other things, other
than those that seem to lodge
their claims.

AMASIKO NOBUNGCALI BAKWANTU

Kutheni lento kusoloko kufuneka ukuba unyamalele,
ungachazanga? Kufutshane ne zibuko lomlambo,
azange sikwazi ukulibona ilitye lizika, inqaba
apho ubu camagusha khona nemi nyanya.

Ibikuphela kwe mvuthuluka yee nwele zakho
ebidada ngaphezu kobuso bomlambo.
Ilanga likhanya, ilizwe lemiMoya lihlangene
nelizimele phantsi kwamanzi –

sasingafuni ukunikezela ngawe. Ngoku
ke lamagubu ahlanza ingoma
engenasiphelo anomnqweno woku
kukhweba ubuyele emva. Kananjalo
nala mahobe, endanda phezu
kwa lemithana inameva, aya
ngxengxeza, zikhulule koo Mamlambo.

Umlindo nomxhentso wakwaNtu, intlombe,
sekukuphela kwendlela yokuhlanganisa
imiMoya. Iminikelo esize nayo, ingoma
engapheliyo esibhidliza amazinyo ngayo,
ube wena uli ciko le ngoma –
zonke zinyibilikela kule ngoma
ingenasiphelo ye ntshabalalo yakho:
isiqingatha esi ngumntu, isiqingatha
esingu Moya.

Ekubuyeni kwakho,
asinazinjongo sokubona wena

uvumisa ngesiphelo see Ndlela
zethu ebomini, mhlawumbi unika
umkhombandlela wesiqalo esitsha –
kumanxweme angaziwayo
ziinkumbulo zethu.

Sonwabe kakhulu kwisimo
esikuso namaza agqumayo
adiliza iziseko zee ntlanti
zethu ngokungena sisini

RITES OF PASSAGE

Why should you always leave
us, unannounced? By the river's
bank, we could not see the stone
sinking, the fort from where
you spoke with the spirits. Only

the brim of your hair sailed
above the river's face. Shining,
the spirit world fused with
the waters –

we would not deliver you. And now
the timeless drums wish to lure
you back. Even the pigeons,
flocking upon these acacias, they
plead, relinquish yourself from
the river people.

The vigil dance, *intlombe*,
seems to be the only meeting
ground. The offerings we have
brought, the transient song
we murmur, as you fluently sing –
all melt into the seamless tune
of your doom: half-human,
half-spirit.

Upon your return,
we do not wish to see you
divine the end of our courses

in life, and perhaps foretell
a new beginning –
along shores foreign
to our memory.

We are much happy to be
who we are and the tides
that billow-encroach
our enclosures in such
a merciless mode.

UMTSHAKAZI OTHINJIWEYO

Ngokuchaphaza kwe langa namhlanje
Bekufanele ukuba kudala ndayishiya le ndawo
Iindawo ezikude
Intlanganisela nabantu bakowethu
Kudala zalibala ngam
Ebutsheni bentsuku zam zobufazi
Ndemka, ndikhangela ubuhlanti bakho.

Zininzi iinyanga endizibalileyo
Ukukhanya obuphanyazayo buginya
Abaninzi kwezo ndonga zidilikileyo
      phezu kwemi lambo
Apho, njengezibulo lo wakowenu umthonyama
Bendili gqirha eli lawula
Imicimbi yakho emininzi.

Izihlwele
Kudala zakushiya ngasemva
Iinyanda ezi nkulu zama chiza bezi thwale
      entloko
Izizwe zilandela emva kwabo
Imihlambi engabalekiyo isasaziwe
Kwezo ntili zilele phesheyea komlambo.

Iinyanga ezilikhulu zindigubungele ngoku
Ndisolusa iinkomo zika yihlo
Ndingomba ama gubu akho enziwe
      ngee mfele
Ndidiniwe, ndixwaye itasi yakho yama chiza
Phezu kwamagxa am akhuthukileyo.

Umyeni wam owamoyisayo
Walibala kudala
Ngobushushu bamabele am adiniweyo
    kutshanje
Nge tshoba lakho le mfene
Nesidlokolo sakho se lokovane
Uyidilizile iminqweno yabo
Inye into esondeleyo kum
Zimbiza ezichininikayo zi nyembezi
    zam.

Namhlanje
Ndifuna wazi ithongo lam lokugqibela
Endingakwazanga
Ukulilawula phezu kwee ndlebe zakho
    eziqinileyo
Ndimke, ungandibonanga
Kuba wena akusayi kuze undikhulule.

Ingaba intlawulo yam ayilanelanga
Ithongo elandi zisa apha ndingumtshakazi?
Sondela, sixhentse
Okokugqibela ke ngoku

THE CAPTURED MAIDEN

By early sunrise this day
I should have long deserted this place.
The spaces far away
Together with my people
Have long forgotten the sight of me.
Early in the days of my womanhood
I left, in search of your kraal.

Many moons have I counted
The glimmering light consuming
Many by the weary banks of the river pool
Where, as first born of your kraal,
I have been master
Of your many ceremonies.

Legions
Long have they deserted you
Big piles of herbs their awards
Crowds behind them
Countless herds scattered
Throughout those sleeping valleys.

Patterning yourself after your predecessors
You suffocated me with your misplaced proverbs
The traditional conclave –
Your main residence
Has lost its relevance.

It is almost a hundred moons now
With me tendering your cattle

And me creating your music
Slouching with your medicinal bag
Over my tattered shoulders.

My defeated husband
Has long forgotten
The warmth of my now tired breasts.
I have to please your kindred
With all that I am.

The members of my clan
And those of my traded-in man
Have long been calling me
Through many dreams –
Gushing words from beyond.

With your baboon fly-whisk
And your chameleon head-gear
Have you shrugged their wishes
I could only own
Countless drums of my tears.

Today
I would like you to know
The contents of my last dream
Which I could not pour
Over your stone ears –
To leave you, unseen
For you would never release me.

Have I not paid enough
For the dream that brought me here?

Come, let us dance
For the last time now.

UMTHWALI WAMAQANDA ENCINIBA WASE KALAHARI

Mfazi
Amaqanda angamashumi amabini enciniba
ajinga emqaleni wakho
Isinga lexolo lomthi libhijelwe kumqolo
wakho
Lizivalile ii ntshukumo zakho
Likucinezele.

Iminxeba erhanqe wonke umqolo
wakho
Ikhandwe kumagqabi omileyo
Echiza lesiNtu iMpundu
Umfuziselo we dyokhwe
ne ngcinezelo
Egqabhuka kumacandelo
ngamacandelo obuntu bakho.

Njengentlaninge yabantwana
Inamathele kumqolo wakho
Amaqanda enciniba agrunjiweyo
emilebeni
Inzala ye ntlabathi etshisayo
yase Kalahari
Umbindi wee Zizwe ne Mpucuko
eya tshabalalayo.

Amaqanda angamashumi amabini
Ezimpuphuma ngamanzi alotywe
ngemizi
Itywina elenziwe ngomthi
liwavalele
Amaselwa wena ongaseliyo
kuwo
Imithombo engayanelisiyo
imizwa yakho.

La maqanda
Imithuba yawo yomile
Iimpuphuma zezibeleko
ezishenxisiweyo
Ezingazange zigagane
nobu mveku bazo
Nangoku
Amaceba amaqanda
ophukileyo ahlanganisiwe.

Izacholo zamaceba amaqanda
ee nciniba
E jika jika abe yhimi tidili
yokuxhentsa
Egcinelwe imicimbi
engcwalisekileyo
Equkunjelwa kwii ngoma
ezi philisayo zee Mboni
Ikhapha imixhentso
ne mibono ebiza imvula.

OSTRICH EGG CARRIER OF THE KALAHARI

Woman
Twenty ostrich eggs hang from your neck
Sinew net tied around your back
Holding you against yourself
Pressing you down.

The threads that run parallel
to your back
Patterned from dried-up leaves
From the African spear plant
Symbol of yoke and bondage
From your many life manifestations.

Like many children
Clinging to your back
Perforated ostrich eggs
Offs-springs of the hot Kalahari sands
Epicentre of eclipsed civilizations.

Twenty ostrich eggs
Full of reed-syphoned water
Vegetal twine plug sealing them off
Calabashes that you never drink from
Springs that never quench your thirst.

With their placentas dried up
Displaced embryos
That could never see their infancy
Still
Broken pieces pierced together.

Ornamental ostrich eggshell beads
Metamorphosing into dance rattles
Reserved for esoteric activities
Culminating into curative shaman songs
Tantalizing rain dances and trances

Abigail Vanessa Bwakila (Tanzania): Poems in Kiswahili

BARUA YA MAPENZI KWA MWANAMKE

Ngozi nyororo kama vile papaso la mtoto wa kiafrica
Macho ya kwenyezayo kope zake ndefu na pana
Hatua kama mwendo wa umeme, taratibu huteleza na mwendo
Pua zitafutazo harufu ya maua

Yeye ni mrembo wa kiafrica
Yeye ni tanzanite ya taifa

Tabasamu ambalo huchoma na kupiga mioyo ya wanaume
Mdomo ujikunjao kama kasoko kubwa
Ile sauti oh jamani ni symphonia
Moyo mwepesi kama vile busu kichwani mwako unapochoka

Yeye ni nuru ya bara
Yeye ni kahawa ya nchi

Kazi zifanyazo wote kuangalia
Husimama hakatisha miendo yao kuangalia kwenye kiza na mvuke
Hukuzungusha na kukunyanyua juu daima
Ngozi tamu kama upeo rasharasha zidondokazo kutokana na mg'arisho wa asali

Yeye ni umande wa asubuhi katika siku
Yeye ni miale joto ya jua hujiamini hata kutikisa mfalme
Nimtazamo husio wa bandia
Ni huzini kwako yeye aondoayo

Ni usiku wa usingizi mwema ni asubuhi njema

Yeye ni mvua kwenye joto la jangwani
Yeye ni utulivu baada ya dhoruba
Kumbatio la kusisimua
Neema isiyo weza angushwa
Yeye anayewindwa na sasa anawinda
Matumaini yote na ndoto zote zimetolewa kwako
mwenyenyekevu wa sura

Yeye ni viungo kwa kila chakula
Yeye ni radi ifuatayo ngurumo
Yeye ni mrembo wa kiafrica
Yeye ni fahari ya bara
Yeye ni umande wa asubuhi katikasiku
Yeye ni mvua kwenye joto la jangwani

Yeye ni wewe
Yeye ni mimi
Yeye ni sisi
Sisi ni yeye

A LOVE LETTER TO A WOMAN

Skin as soft as the touch of Africa's love child
Eyes that bat their lashes glad and wide
Steps like an electric slide, oh so gently slip and slide
A nose that hunts the smell of tulips

She is the African beauty
She is the nation's Tanzanite

A smile that pierces and strikes the hearts of men
A mouth that arches like the great crater
That voice, oh my, a symphony
Heart as light as the kisses she bestows atop your weary head
She is the continents' pride
She is the country's coffee bean

Deeds that cause all to gaze
Stop in their tracks and stand in a cloudy, steamy haze
Spin you round and trip you up; an ever winding maze
Skin as succulent, mhm, as a dripping, drooling honey glaze

She is the days' morning dew
She is the suns warm rays

The confidence to make kings shake
The attitude she does not fake
The sorrow from you she will take
Your goodnights' sleep, your fresh awake

She is the rain in scotching dessert

She is the calm after the storm

Her thrilling embrace
No such fall from grace
She is the hunted, now commence the chase
All hopes, all dreams, bestowed upon one humble face

She is the spice to every meal
She is lightning to accompanying thunder

She is the African beauty
She is the continents pride
She is the day's morning dew
She is the rain in scorching dessert

She is you
She is me
She is us
We are her

KUCHUKUA HISA

Sina vingivya kutoa, kukopesha au kukodisha
Ila ninamajibu potofu tayari kwa mashindano ya urembo
Na ukweli ulioharibika wenye ulemavu
Nina visa kidogo ambayo huwa hainiangushi
Nina barakoa nyingi za kuficha uso wangu na mawasawaso kama vazi la jioni

Sina mengi ila visanamu mwanasesere vilivyofinyuka vikishikana mikono kujiwakilisha uwepo wao, jana, leo na kesho

Sina mengi yakuonyesha, ila sumu tamu iliyoisha muda wake wa kuarithirika, sina mengi ila hewa ya sumu ndani ya mapafu yangu
Damu ndani ya mishipa yangu na ngoma zikishindana ndani ya kifua changu

Nina konde mbili na kifua kilichopigwa pampu tayari kila wakati kwa vita iliyokusudiwa milele kushindwa
Nina macho yaonayo zaidi ya miaka yangu na ndoto
Nina tiketi ya show mbaya, mwingizaji ni mimi mie na mi

Nina wakaaji ndani ya kichwa changu na majitu yakutisha chini ya kitanda changu
Ninamachozi yaliyo gandishwa vifurushi tayari kwa kuuza
Zina kuja kwa idadi, ninatengeneza vizuri

STOCK TAKING

I do not have much to give away or lend or rent
All I have are beauty pageant ready lies
And disfigured, disabled truths
I've got pretty cocktails that only ever let me down
Many masks to hide my face and delusions for an evening gown

I do not have much but miniature shrunken down dolls holding hands, the future, past and present representations of self

I do not have much to show
But tasty poisons well past their expiration dates
I do not have much, but the toxic air in my lungs
The blood in my veins and the drums in concert on my chest

I have two fists and pumped chest
Ready as ever for a battle I am forever destined to lose
I have eyes that see beyond my years and dreams
I have a ticket to a grim show starring me, myself and I

I have occupants in my head
And monsters under my bed
I have frozen tears packaged to sell
They come in numbers, I make them well

WAKATI EPIFANIA INAPOKUJA

Nimezama kwenye moto
Nimeunguzwa kwenye maji
Nimesikia kungatwa na jino la nyoka
Nikatumia ukombozi kama kitanzi
Nikatembea juu ya maji
Nimeweka sumu kwenye mito
Nimekaa juu ya mawingu
Nime hubiri uongo
Nimeeneza wivu
Nimeongea ukweli
Nimezungumza mawazo yangu

Nimewaingiza ndani wale wasio ruhusiwa kuingizwa
Nimependa zaidi ya neema kwa wakati
Nimejaza maumivu makali katikati ya kifua changu
Nimekuwa kero ya wadudu wazembe
Nimetabasamu wakati wote nilipokuwa na hamu ya kulia
Nilitoa machozi matamu na machungu yaliyo jaa furaha
Nilitazama juu ya uso wa kiumbe
Nikaona kesho yangu na nikaona jana yangu
Nilivaa taji na nikavua taji
Halafu nikachoma himaya ya kifalme
Nikawafukuza walowezi

Nimeishi kwenye ukimya
Nikiwa hai peke yake kwenye mawazo yangu
Unakaza mdundo wa moyo wangu
Najua mimi nina toka mwanzoni, kabla ya uwepo wangu
Nimeona miaka katika ufahari wake
Nimepima huzuni na nimehesabu nyuso zilizo kunjwa

Nimehesabu maumivu ya moyo
Juu ya kuona yote hayo
Bado nachagua kuwepo kwangu
Isingelikuwa bila maumivu ya kuchosa nisengeweza kujua
furaha ya ukweli ninini
Nakama si kivuli cha mvua
Jua linge wezaje waka tena?

Nimezama kwenye moto
Nimeunguzwa kwenye maji
Nimesikia kungatwa na jino la nyoka
Nikatumia ukombozi kama kitanzi
Nikatembea juu ya maji
Nimeweka sumu kwenye mito
Nimekaa juu ya mawingu
Nime hubiri uongo
Nimeeneza wivu
Nimeongea ukweli
Nimezungumza mawazo yangu

Nimeona kesho yangu na nikaona jana yangu
Nilivaa taji na nikavua taji

Yote haya kabla dunia haijawa
Yote haya wakati bado mmelala

WHEN AN EPIPHANY CAME

I've drowned in fire
Burned in water
Felt the sting of the serpent's tooth
Use redemption as a noose
I've walked on water
Poisoned rivers
Sat on a cloud
Preached lies
Spread envy
Spoke the truth
Spoke my mind

I've let those in who I should not
I've loved beyond the grace of time
I've filled that dull ache amidst my chest
Been a nuisance- an idling pest
I've smiled when all I desired was to cry
Shed sweet and sour tears of bountiful joy
Looked upon the creature's face
Seen my future, seen my past
Worn the crown then shed the crown
Then burned the kingdom
Banished the settlers

I've lived in the silence
Only attuned to my thoughts
Crammed the rhythm of my heart
Known who I was from the very start
For before I came into existence
I saw the years in all their splendour

I measured the sorrow
I counted the frowns

Tallied the heartaches
For upon looking at it all
Still I chose to exist
For if not for the tedious ache
How could I know what joy truly is

And if not for the shadow of rain
How could the sun then shine again

I've drowned in fire
Burned in water
Felt the sting of the serpent's tooth
Use redemption as a noose
I've walked on water
Poisoned rivers
Sat on a cloud
Preached lies
Spread envy
Spoke the truth
Spoke my mind

Seen my future, seen my past
Worn the crown, then shed the crown
All before the world began
All while you were sleeping still

15 AUGUSTI 2021

Piga ngumi kwenye koo
Piga kwenye tumbo
Huruma kidogo hapa na pale

Nimeweka muda wa uponyaji
Kwa neema nikakubali
Lakini kama vile moyo wangu ulirudisha mdundo sahihi
Kama vile nilivyoanza kukumbuka jinsi ya kuhema
Pumzi moja ndani, pumzi moja nje
Umefumba macho yako yaliyochoka, kamwe hutaweza fungua tena

Nimepiga mapigo ya moyo ya dunia
Nimechukua viunzi na kutengua mbavu
Nimepasua ardhi na ikanimeza mzima
Nimeenda tafuta roho yako nzuri
Napitia miaka ya makaa ya mawe yanayowaka
Kamwe bila kulalamika
Kamwe bila kupoteza koona lengo
Machozi yanatirizika, sasa mifereji ya machozi yanatoa damu
Weka aibu kwa mafuriko ya kale
Wito wa nguvu zilizopo

Kuna kosa kwenye mfumo wako
Kunakijishimo kwenye mipango yako
Umefanya kosa kubwa na mie pekee sija pendezwa

Nikupe nini badili yake kwa malipo?
Nafsi kwa nafsi, hii ndio hisa?
Na kwa vile ninavyo miliki, hakika utachukua

Umefanya makosa makubwa

Nikazungusha mikono duniani
Nikiwezesha kusimamisha haraka
Mate usoni lakini bado inatembea kuirahisi
Muda usimame, onyesha kutopuuzwa

Wakati yote yameshindikana
Wakati ngozi yangu iliyochujika nanga katikamifupa
Wakati nilipiga kelele kwauchungu "siwezi kusamehe"
Wakati nimetoa yote kwa huzuni na akachukua zaidi ya mgao wa haki
Nikatulia na hatia bandia yakutokubalika
Ila haitakuwa sawa

Yote yaliyobaki ni kumbukumbu na tabasamu
Ile hisia ya furaha ya ukweli unapoingia kichwani mwangu kilichochanganyika
Unaponitembelea, unapoongea, unapokuja kwa kikombe cha chai kitulizacho

Hii yatosha, hii yaniletea faraja mimi
Ilimradi nina muda wa utulivu
Ilimradi nina ishi, wewe vile vile utaishi kupitia kwangu
Na hata kama mimi vile vile nitaondoka hii nchi tambarare
Utakuwa hai ndani ya kifo kama ulivyo kuwa katika maisha yako

Wewe sasa uko kwa wasiokufa
Umehifadhiwa, umeheshimika, umekumbukwa, umethaminiwa
Mpaka hiyo siku tutakapoonana tena

Nakupenda wewe sasa, nakupenda bado, nakupenda daima

15TH AUGUST 2021

Punched in the throat
Struck in the gut
A little empathy here and there

Allocated some healing time
Graciously I accepted
But just as my heart regained its normal rhythm
Just as I began to remember how to breathe
One breath in, one breath out
You closed your tired eyes never to open them once more

I struck the beating heart of the Earth
I took shears and separated its ribcage
I ruptured the ground and it swallowed me whole
Went in search for your beautiful soul
Walked through years of burning coal
Never once relenting
Never once losing sight of the goal

Tears ran out, now my ducts produced blood
Putting to shame the ancient flood
Summoning the powers that be

There's a fault in your system
A nook in your plan
You've made a terrible mistake and I for one am not a fan

What can I give you in return?
A soul for a soul, is that the stake?
Then the one I possess you will surely take
You've made a terrible mistake

I wrapped my arms around the world
I made it come to a heading halt
A spit in the face that it all simply proceeds
Time must stop, show some respect
Everything stagnant, show no neglect

When all else failed
When my skin sloughed off its anchor bone
When I screamed in anguish "this I will never condone"
When I gave all to grief and she took more than her fair share
I settled into a guilt ridden pseudo acceptance. But we will never be square

All that's left—memories, smiles
That feeling of genuine happiness
As you pop into my cluttered head
For a visit, for a talk, for a cup of soothing tea

This is enough, this comforts me
For as long as I have our quiet moments
For as long as I live, you too shall live through me
And even after I too depart this Earthly plain
You shall be even more alive in death as you were in life

You are now immortalized
Preserved, revered, remembered, cherished

Until such day we meet again
I love you now, I love you still, I love you always

MTI WA ASUBUHI

Niko na amani niko vitani
Mie ni ukimya kwenye mkusanyiko
Mie ni furaha chini ya machozi yatetemekayo
Mie ni alama ya maafa
Mie ndiye kosa kati ya nyota ipofushayo
Mie ndiyo hofu amabayo ungekuwanayo
Ni chombo kamili ungependa kukichukia
Ni hatima uliyoipuuza
Ni damu iliyo mwagika, ni maumivu uliyoyazika
Mimi ni alfajiri iliyotanda wekundu uliotokana na nyasi
Mtoaji uzima, mtoaji wa sadaka
Mie ni dhambi na mie ni ungamo
Ni wakutolewa, wakujisalimisha
Ni sauti iliyopunguzwa ikiamuru songa mbele
Kivuli ambacho unasikia kimefungwa juu ya bega lako
Nimaono katika upofu
Mie nikilakitu ambacho kiliwahi kuwa na vilevile bado haitakuwa
Kifo katika maisha pekee, uhuru wa kifo kutolewa murua

MOTHER TREE

I am peace and I am war
I am the silence in a crowd
I am the joy beneath trembling tear
I am the master of disaster
I am the fault amidst blinding star
I am the dread you could have had
The entity you love to hate
The fate you ignore
The blood you shed, the pain you buried
I am the red dawn departed from Hyades
The giver of life, the sacrifice delivered
I am sin and I am confession
The release in surrender
The dampened voice beckoning you forward
The shadow you feel cradled over your shoulder
The sight in blindness
I am everything that ever was and yet will never be

Aliker p'Ocitti (Uganda): Poems in Acholi (Luo)

Kec Opoko Kin Gweno Ki Okwata

Con ki con, Gweno ki Okwata
Onongo gi bedo kacel
Ento kec obin opoto
Ma min Gweno pe tongo bollo.
Min Gweno oceto wii oduu
Kayenyo gin acama me otyenu.
Uketo lodii ma ki onyo iwii oduu
Lodii omako mac ci ogamo lum
Mac owango ot pa Okwata woko.
Ikare ma Okwata okok pi ot mere
Ni Gweno omyero oyub ot mere
Gweno ogamo ni Okwata okok ikum kec.

How Famine Brought a Rift between the Hen and Eagle

Long, long time ago; the Hen and the Eagle
Lived together as one community.
When famine befell their community
The Hen could never share with its chicks.
The Hen visited a pit to look for food
While there, it uncovered burning coal
That had been dumped in the pit
And it lit grass that burnt the Eagle's nest
When the Eagle asked the Hen
To rebuild its nest to rest
The Hen replied the Eagle
To blame its fate
On famine.

Kwoo Pa Okwata

Pe pa ot oweko Okwata tiku tuk atuka
Labongo pye piny bot min Gweno.
Pe pa ot opoko kin min Gweno ki Okwata
Oweko min Gweno ki Okwata odoko lumone.
Me culu wang kwoo pi wangoo ot pa Okwata
Okwata ocako kwalo lutino gweno.
Kare ki kare, Okwata tingo latin gweno
Tuk kede wa malo ma min Gweno pe nongo
Man, weng loka kec ma opoto con ki con.

The Eagle's Vengeance

In vengeance, the Eagle started to snatch chicks
for being cursed by the Hen to fly in the sky.
When the Eagle snatches a chick, it flies high
For the Hen never ever to reach it
And feeds on it as its food.

Lam Pa Min Gweno

Min Gweno olamo Okwata pi kwalo lutino ne
Oweko Okwata buttu iwii yat.
Apoka poka man ikin min Gweno ki Okwata
Oweko min Gweno gwoko lutine ite ywete ka oneno Okwata

The Hen's Curse

The Hen then cursed the Eagle to live on a tree like other wild birds.
This is why the Hen protects its chicks under its feathers Whenever it sees an Eagle flying in the sky.

Oscar Gwiriri (Zimbabwe): Poems in chiShona

Nyarara

Nyika ino izere vangwaru nemafuza.
Ariko mafuza anopikisa chakanaka.
Variko vangwaru vanotsigira chakaipa.
Iwe kana wati koso pamunamato, chingonyarara.
Varipo vangwaru nemafuza vacharakashana,
Vamwe vachimira newe, vamwe vachikushoropodza.
Pane vachaitenga nyaya kuita yavo,
Vagoipambira, kuikwatisa, kumona nekuishinyirisa,
Votsapfurana nekupfatsurirana kure senyoka.
Potse potse kutozobatana kwiyo pahuro,
Asi iwe nyakukosora pamunamato, wakanyarara.
Siya vapedzerane mataka avo nenyaya yako,
Vagara vange vachishaya gwenya redaka ravo.
Inzwa ini, kunyarara kuno kunda zvose pasi pano!

Be Calm

There are plenty of the wise and foolish,
Fools who object whatever is good,
The wise who stand for the evil,
Even if you have erred, just be still,
There are fools and the wise, who will argue,
Others in support yet others are against you.
There are those good at hacking hurt,
They will propel and reinvigorate the case,
Such that they will fight over it uninvited,
To an extend of stirring hatred and war,
Yet you who strayed would be quite about it.
Just let them solve their grudge over your case,
Their differences were just awaiting a trigger,
Get it from me; silence is the root of peace.

Ngavararame zvavo

Varipo vanhu vatinotyira
Kuti vakafa, nyika inofawo.
Variko vanhu vatinotyira
Kuti vakafa, vanondozadza denga.
Varipo vanhu vatinotyira
Kuti vakafa, vanondoshaisha ngirozi.
Varipo vanhu vatinotyira
Kuti vakafa, vanondotengesa denga.
Varipo vanhu vatinotyira
Kuti vakafa, vanondotenga denga.
Varipo vanhu vatinotyira
Kuti vakafa, vanondosvibisa midzimu.
Varipo vanhu vatinotyira
Kuti vakafa, vangazoita yedu midzimu.
Varipo vanhu vatinotyira
Kuti vakafa, vanondodhiriza gehena.
Varipo vanhu vatinotyira
Kuti vakafa, vanozotonga denga nepasi.
Varipo vanhu vatinotyira
Kuti vakafa, kudenga hakuchaendeki.

Let them live

There is such kind of people we are afraid,
Whom if they die, the world also dies.
There are people for whom we fear
That if they die, they will colonise heaven.
There are there whom we worry about
That if in heaven, they may even rape angels.
There are people we're concerned about
That they may corruptly dispose of heaven.
They are there those we are scared
That when they die, they'll own heaven's title deeds.
There are people whom we are worried about
That when they die, they will corrupt sacred ancestors,
We're anxious they will become our profane ancestors.
There are those kind of people we're apprehensive that
When they die they will break hell loose.
There are people whom we are petrified that
When they die they will rule heaven and earth.
There are people were are skeptical about that
Upon their death, heaven becomes out of bounds.

Kuchema nakuchema

Nhasi tiri kuchema gwenyambira Stella Chiweshe Nekati,
Nezuro takaviga magamba emimhanzi.
Dzwana takadzichengeta hwereshenga dzekunyora.
Svondo rapera takavakotsa vatambi vemitambo.
Mwedzi wapera takatsira mhizha.
Mwaka nemwaka tichingotorerwa nyanzvi.
Zvotoperazve pasina agoka unyanzvi hwedu!
Mitambo netsika zvozvotokuva semazhanje!
Vapwere gamuchirai chimwenje chotokupai ichi,
Pasi ringasara risina anokwenya chero mbira nenduri.
Zvakwangove kuchema nakuchema pasi rino.

Mourning and mourning

We are mourning Stella Chiweshe Nekati,
Yesterday we buried our famous singers,
The day before it was our prolific writers,
Last week, we bid life to familiar sports persons,
Last month it was also professional artists,
Season by season we lost the talented ones,
Yet none would have taken the skills baton,
Sports and culture extinct like out-seasoned fruits,
Oh children of today please take a lesson,
Otherwise this world will be uncultured.
Oh it's mourning after mourning time and again!

Rudo rweDandemutande

Hezvo!
Usandiitire manenji akagochwa iwe!
Han'ya naani zvangu munhu akazvarwa.
Usada kuti nywee nywee nywee,
Uchiita sewakandiona mukereke.
Takasangana padandemutande shamwari!
Inga waitoona ndichidiwawo chaizvo?
Ndatombokuitirawo zvangu mutsa wekukuda!
Wave kuda kutondifurufusha nekundifudza!
Kundirambidza kuswera padandemutande kuti zvaita sei?
Hapasipo pawakandionera here nhai iwe?
Saka deno ndaisawepo waizondiwanira kupi?
Ini handidi munhu ane udzvanyiriri ini.
Kana iwe wakauyapo uchitsvaga mukadzi,
Chiziva kuti ini ndaitove chidziva chepo.
Tisu takaritanga dare riye pauzima.
Saka haundiudziri pekuswera nekusaswera.
Iwe ziva nekufara kuti ndiwe uneni,
Michohwe yepadaremutande unei nayo?
Ndochitadza kufara manje nekuda kwako?
Ewo, kana iriyo imba yacho ngaigare zvayo!
Ini handisi kuzobuda mudare iroro.
Kana zvakusvota enda unofa.

Online Affairs

Oh my God!
Please don't shock me!
Why worry, beautiful as I am?
Don't irritate me with rebukes,
As if we met each other in church,
Remember we were group chatters,
And you witnessed members' proposals.
Having done you this sweet favour of love,
How come you are then stalking me like that?
And denying me from chatting on social media,
Isn't it where we got to know each other after all?
Had it not been social media, would you be with me?
I am skeptical of women oppressors my dear.
If you joined the group searching for a lover,
Be aware that I had been existing there ever since,
I am a pioneer administrator of that socio-group,
You can't just wake up regulating my membership,
Be proud that I am dating you after and above all,
Why bother about social media pranks and flirts?
Should I not enjoy my freedom all because of you?
If that's what marriage isn't meant to be, let it be.
I am not going to exit that chatting group my dear.
If it doesn't auger well with you, then go hang.

Kudetemba

Detembo manzwi anokuma,
Ivo asina kunyorwa kana kutaurwa.
Nhetembo mwana ari mudumbu
Ramai vakoniwa kusvotora mimba.
Nduri inyika iri kurwirwa rusununguko
Iyo yakasununguka kurwa kusati kwatanga.
Nhetembo madetembedzo easingatauri.
Nheketerwa inzwi riri kutekenyedza nzeve dzeasinganzwi
Madetembedzo ndiwe neni tisinganzwisisi zvatinonzwa.
Nyanduri musutswi anoronga manzwi aasingagone kufunga.
Kudetemba kurutsa musvo wepfungwa pauzima zvisina ukoni.

Poetry

Poetry is words bellowing,
Yet unwritten nor spoken.
Poetry is a child in a womb,
Who silently resisted abortion.
Poesy is a country fighting for freedom,
Yet it won before it commenced war.
Poetry is words rolling in the dumb's mouth.
Poetry is words oscillating in a deaf's ear.
It's you 'n'me misunderstanding understanding.
A poet is a smith arranging words he can't think of.
Praise poetry vomits deep thinking without ado.

Ndinodei?
Kana ndiri kwaChivi kubasa,
Ndinoshuvira kuve kuMacheke kumba.
Kana ndiri kuMacheke pamutambarakede,
Ndinoshuvira kuve kwaChivi kumutokodo.
Dai zvikasazodaro ndave kudenga,
Ndoshuvira kuve zvangu mugehena!

What do I want?

When I am in Chivi
I long for sweet home Macheke.
When I am in Macheke, relaxing,
I wish to be in Chivi, at work.
I hope it won't be just like that,
Longing for hell whilst in heaven.

Aisha Hussaina Idris Manarakis (Nigeria): Poems in Nupe

WUN A FE KPANDARA ZAKANMA

Kpandara tsutsu ye kpeye a
Aga e kpe u ye kpe, ezadecizhi a le nbo foga
Nda toh Nna a bici rayi a zhi atatoh nya egizhi
Bona nuwan lebaye, wunde kagbo, wunde yekodaci kanma
Wunman e ye kangwa a

Kaaasa! Wo le kendo nuwan fe dazan da
Ci gba zadecizhi lo na ye
Wo le kendo karazhi gbinti na ye
Kashi kendo lenbuko ku emizhi ku na,
Wo leye a?
Kagan u jin kpandara tsutsu ade zana lenbuko a tsun nbo na a
Ade Nda, Nna toh egi na wun a de la na a
Afe emi kokoro tsa wun a ku o

Wo fedun kpaye le a ni
Wunga yi kpandara wotso yi nana o na?
Wode kagbo ko egwakanci?

Cin kendo ezazhi bici rayi da kpe fiti Sokowunba o na le de
Na kpandara tsutsu ao na, ka ahtso a gbinti fi lenbuko
Yebonci sukun na Soko tswa ta kata ti o na
Nna na feta eti cigban lenbu ci fe gba be egi na sukun?

Mi, woe toh yi kpata wunga yi kpandara yi nyi o
Yi a go foga gan a bona kpandara tsutsu ye kangwa ya a
Wunman dokun kakanyi.

THE BRIDGE OF MORTALITY FOR MANY

A bridge of death,
shrouded in mystery
and fate's dark veil
If its path were foreseeable, families would abandon their homes
Parents would fiercely fight for their lives
and those of their precious wards
For this force is relentless, piercing, and has many channels to claim

Oh, didn't you witness the waters
surge with deadly momentum?
How it devoured families whole, swallowed properties, and swept houses away?
Didn't you see the mighty flood's merciless hand?
If not for the bridge to death, the flood would have met desolate streets
It wouldn't have claimed
the father, mother,
or the innocent child
Only empty buildings would have stood,
solitary and still

Have you ever sat on the precipice of reflection?
If this bridge
were your destined path
to eternity?

See how some sought refuge on the rooftop of place of worship
Yet, it became the bridge
to their demise,
consumed by the raging tide?

What of the blind man,
saved on the rooftop's fragile perch?
Or the woman clinging to wooden debris,
her baby held tight?
Myself, you, and all of us, if this were our bridge
to death
We wouldn't have survived that fateful day
For the bridge of death
is unforgiving,
with many doors to unending consumption.

NYIZAGI NA E JINBO BAGI NA

Nyizagi nana a fe ryatwa bologi
Wun a fe u ebawuci tsakagi
Be yegborolo waci wangi

Woga, de Nna wunci kpe etan egi u
Wun e kpe toh nya zakan ye man
Kanga ga wun e de nya eza go man o

Woci a fe nuwan sangi na zakanma e toh fin na
Wo a fe goga na zakanma e to fu na
Wo a fe o gbanciko na zakanma e fa wuru na

Nyagbandeci nini na gan nyagbandeci kanma na
Nna na dan New York o, egwa bibajinre u ma e tun Najeriya
Atatoh yizhe fyanyi na

Woga le u ye wo a gbin gan etun guru za a
Wo a gbingan ebojin wangi za a
Wo a gbingan nyagban eza gowo za a

Wuntso yi bokun, nyagban u yi ta o
Woga go etsan yikan bokun be u nyi, wo a de zandoci la ya a
Bona ryatwa bologi u yi yayi nyi o

Kube ninma efo yina e,
Nna zakanma, Nna Hussaina Idris Manarakis
Nna Amb. Abdullah Alh. Abubakar
Nna kun wawazhi; Lady B. Bless

A WOMAN WITH AN ACT OF A MAN

She's a beautiful gift
A revered mentor
And a good promoter

If a mother adores her own children
She'll adore even those that are not hers
And only then she's called a true mother

She's a stream, quenching the thirst of many
A well, benefiting many
A full blown tree, shading many

One philanthropist, equivalent to thousand
A mother based in New York yet her hands reach both far and near

Her attributes reflect her big heart
Even in her character
And in her patience

Her heart as pure as dove
Her smile always radiates
Because she's our heavenly gift

Happy birthday to you
Mother to all, even to Hussaina Idris Manarakis
Mother to Amb. Abdullah Alh. Abubakar
A mother to many children; Lady B. Bless

YETU YI DANBO

Yiga e kpa enya guru
Yiga e ba enya guru
Yiga e tu etun guru ye
Yiga e wa ebanzhe
Wangi ya kin nyaba yi na.

Kin Najeriya yina
Lu na a zhe yeka
Wun a fe na zafu nna hadizhi e
Gangan u na anma
Be yetu wangizhi wunga a ge.

Yina yi efo woro
Etswa woro nya
Eya woro be
Ebanzhe zhi
Toh yetu zhi.

Najeriya sanle a gwa tu manpa
Agbin u gan na
Wungan wangi e ba wun ni
Bona eyi wunciko
Wun yi o na Nusa tsuwozhi la shishi na.

Wo man ga cin u le
Ebanzhe zhi danbo
Bona wunjin na a jin
Tsuwo na e jin yina a.

Eni na a ko tsuwo na a
Zo tsuwo, yiga ko nya
Yinana wunma u gan
Nya tsuwo bona
Yi wagan etun nusa
Nazhi gogan na u kpebo a
Anma be yekpa guru i
Toh yetu wangizhi.

THERE'S STILL HOPE

When goodness is our heartfelt wish,
When prayers for prosperity echo through the skies,
When anticipation of brighter days fuels our soul,
And when we yearn for fortune's gentle hand to bless our beloved land.

Nigeria, a nation of paradox, where hope and despair entwine,
A land of contrasts, where dreams are forged in resilience,
Though many voices whisper discontent, our optimism will prevail.

Today marks a rebirth, a dawn of promise and renewed dreams,
A fresh month unfolds,
Bringing change
And revitalized hope's sweet refrain.

The melody of yesterday's songs has faded into the night of yesterday,
Let's compose a new harmony, more enchanting and soothing than the last,
For we refuse to let the pioneering spirit of our past heroes be in vain;
Instead, we'll nurture positive thoughts
And optimism's radiant flame.

EFO YIZHELE

Efona
Mi wa zabaci za
Na min a gangan, baza abe le yizhe benyi na

Ezabaci
Eya
Gangbajinci abe epagiyaci na

Ezabaci
Na min wa ci yakpe na

Anma foga a fe u
Efona ezan yizhele min a zheban na
Efona a eyekosun min toh nyagban min ya be giye binbiri na

Ngba, mi ca wo be
Na min a tukpa etsan yikan woro be na
Na a yi be wiwa enya e ko bibajinre a na?

Ngba, mi de zaeni wo
Na a be, ci ga min lugwa dan ngakpeti o zunmago nyi a na?

Ngba, egiye tsaka
Nana zheban lo ninma nyagbanfa wo?

Min ga a nana
Ci a eyewu eni managi, na esun a be benyi na.

A DAY TO LIVE...

That day
I was buried in the need of a partner
To talk, share and live with

A partner
A friend
Adviser and motivator

The partner
I love and really rely on

But it was the day
My journey changed
The day left my eyes and depth of heart
Filled with boiling tears

Can I start over
And build a new smile
Not around my need and help?

Can I find one
Who will not come with a bag of disappointment at last?

Can that flowing water
Change to air of joy?

I must stand focused
And relish the new song of the bright future.

EGWAFIN YA YEGBOROLO

Egi Nupe ga le Nna ye
Wun e sa u gan kube lazhin i
Wunga le Nda u ye
Kube yigidi
Wunga le eba u ye
Yaya kube lozun i
Wunga be le egazhi ye
Ye kube ebo e

Yelo mi yi Nupe
Kinigi mi yi nya gi Nupe
Ede mi yi nya Nupe
Bona ngba ga mi e ta o
Ga man ku yi be zhi na o

Kpasa nana e yi u gan nya Edu
Mi ga u tati o, woci u kpe kpa o
Wun yi esa
Woga u gba shin
Wo a nya Tsankan
Bona ale kpasa nana ye na
Ale Nupe ye

Beacin;

Nya yi danna u la u kperi be nyaba danna e
Nupencizhi a la a zhe nini u la u fe egwafin toh emigun u ya yegborolo

Nupencizhi a wa dozhi a, yi egwafin
Nupencizhi a ba dozhi nyi jinre ci u la u fe yegborolo

Nda mi, ngba egwa nini e la kara lo ti?
Nna mi, ngba egwafin e wa rikpe?
Yegi mi, ngba yegborolo e ye de be wo a lo a mi a lo a nyi
Toh ewo zunma din

Toh ki a la yi ci a fingwa, gunmi ya yegborolo a nyi o?

Ki ayi Nupe Bida, Agaye, toh Lapayi o. Bini
Ki ayi nya Mokwa, Tsaragi toh Patigi o. Gbede
Ki ayi nya Kogi, Basange toh Kakanda o. Kin tako

Nupe Nupe Yi Yi o
Yi gan be rikpe sakpe
Yi fingwa I fedun I tati zongun nini o
Yi gi jekun, kuli toh kunu fin gani
Bona Nupe Kwara, Niger toh Kogi nini yi o.

UNITY FOR PROGRESS

When a Nupe child
Sees her mother,
She greets her
With 'Kube lazhin I'
A warm smile blooms like a sunrise in her eyes
She tells her father 'Kube yigidi'
A term of endearment,
And whispers 'Yaya kube lozun I' to her beloved husband's gentle ear
With visitors, she extends a gracious 'Ye Kube ebo e',
A bridge of respect and warmth

My heritage is Nupe
My roots run deep
My stance is strong
My attire is Nupe, a vibrant tapestry
'Ngba' is my mother tongue, a melody that binds
Assembling us here,
A celebration of our shared identity

This sacred fabric is called Edu, which weaves stories of our past
When placed on my head, and
When draped on the shoulder by you,
It symbolizes beauty that will forever last.
When tied around the waist, it beckons to the rhythmic 'tsankan' dance
A symphony of movement, a testament to our cultural trance,
For whenever the fabrics of Edu is seen,
Nupe is seen, and

Pride shines bright
A symbol of unity, a beacon in the night

Let's shun the shadows of disparity
Nupencizhi, united we stand, for progress and prosperity we strive
When we love and support one another, unity flourishes,
Progress blooms, a garden of hope and promise

Nda mi, we ask
Can one arm lift a load to the head?
Does unity thrive with segregation?
Nna mi, the answer is etched
Yegi mi,
Can we achieve progress with "you won't go if I don't go?"
Let's strategize together, our hearts beating as one
Why can't we unite, our voices raised as one?

What will they call the Nupe from Bida, Agaye, and Lapai? Bini
What about the Nupe from Mokwa, Tsaragi, and Patigi, Gbede
What about the Nupe from Kogi, Basange, and Kakanda, Kin Tako

We are Nupe, let's shun segregation
Let's unite on one mat. Let's break bread together
Let's dine together, sharing jekun, Kuli, and Kunu's creamy delight, for the
Nupe from Kwara, Niger, and Kogi, are
One people
One spirit and

One light

Mujaheed Matashi (Nigeria): Poems in Hausa

Ma'askin Dare

Wani kaɗaici na damu na, shiru yana ta kira na,
In zo mu tauna, kalma da kalma, in ɓoye duk harufana,
Ido da kwallin duhun dare, haka na ɗauki alƙalumana,
Raina ya ce, "zana so a nan ko ka zana hoton kaina",
A kwai kurame a kunnuwa na jira, yininsu da kwana:
Sauti na karar alƙalami in yana kwatancen sufar tufarki.

Fuska ta allo, kamar madubi, tana ta tallan ilimi,
Su tawwada na ta zayyana, mai aman su ne alƙalami,
Shi ko ƙalam na rawa cikin so yana ta ɗaukar ɗigimi,
Can zuciya ke sanar shi me zai saka ta sigar fahami,
Rai nawa ai shi ka yin zuga nan ga zuci sai ta yi ɗumi,
Karshe ashe ke kike wa raina raɗa ki ce masa ya ambace ki.

Ni me na samu? Gare ni komai ya saura duk kin haɗiye,
Ni ba ga sonki ba, ba a bin ki ba, tsaka-tsaki gani tsaye,
Sai dai Zabira kaɗai nake riƙe, cikinta raina ajiye,
Wataran na laluba don in ce sa shi, "Kai daina tsumaye!"
Na iske kin yanka ran da aska, a ɗaure ko ko a giciye,
Kamar ma'askin dare, kin tsaga zuci, adadin rashin ganinki.

The Midnight Barber

A certain loneliness presses me—silence keeps calling,
Urging me to chew on word by word, hiding each letter.
My eyes rimmed with kohl of night, I reach for my pens.
My soul says: 'Draw love here, or sketch the shape of me.'
There, deaf ears await to listen in the hush of day and night
To the sound my pen makes while sketching the shade of your garment.

The face of the slate, like a mirror, reflects the wares of knowledge.
And my ink keeps calligraphing with grace; its bearer, the pen, pours it forth.
And the pen dances in love—showing off in strokes of flair.
There, the heart reveals to the pen what to write through mystical incantation.
But it's my soul that provokes the heart, stirring its heat until it burns.
In the end, it was you all along—whispering to my soul, urging it to speak of you!

What have I gained? All I had was devoured by you.
I neither hold your love, nor trace your steps—merely standing in-between.
I clutch only Zabira[1]—my soul waits in its pouch.
One day, I reached into it—to tell my soul, 'Enough of this longing!'
But I found you had slayed my soul with a razor—left bound or crucified.
Like the midnight barber, you slashed my heart—in pieces, as many as the times I didn't see you.

[1]Hausa traditional Barber's roll.

Gindin Magani

A kwai wasu kalmomi da ba sa cikin littafi,
Manzanni ba sa faɗa, waliyyai ba sa gada,
Mai sauraro ba ya ji, tsokar harshe ba ta faɗi,
Alƙaluma ba su rubutawa, takardu ba su ɗauka,
Ba a mafarkin su, ba a gani ko a tuno su:
Kalmomin Ubangiji ne Ya ɓoye su a bakin mawaƙi.

The Root of the Cure

There are words that books don't hold,
No prophet speaks, no saint foretold.
The listener hears not, tongue stays still,
Pens don't write, nor do pages fill.
They come not in dreams, nor flash to sight—
They're God's own words, sealed in the poet's mouth.

Souad Zakarani (Morocco): Poems in Arabic

حى المنام

أخاف أن أغمض عيناي
يا أماه
ستطرح علي الأسئلة
في عينيك. قلي
تتثاقل الكلمات في فمي
فقد سكنتني بعينيك
انطق يا ايتها الأقاصي
اخرجي مني
لا أريد أن أحملها أكثر
ربما استطيع نفسي
بجسدي تحرر من الأكفان
أرسلها خارج جثتنا
هل اقتربت البيت مرة أخيرة
قبل أن ننزح
هل لنا أن نصروه للذكرى
ونخزن كل ضحكاتنا وبكائنا او صراخنا

71

تنزح
أي للبحر المتراص أمامنا
كعناق خجول
في عالم يسلبنا
هل لك ان ترسل طنينا للمحيطات
المجاورة
ل حوتا عما لقرب قاعدة المضل
هل لنا أن نبتدع أبجية جيدة
للخوف والألم للبيت
تصل العالم لك
الصوت الرمادي التمر فوقنا
طيران طناهدير الصواريخ
فوق خضر فوق دمار
فوق شلا قبر لكمت وب فحمجيت حترق
اثر حزم ناري
لن نقول لهم قنا .. قلنا لهم
ألف متوت شفلل عيون من السماء
و نحن نبحث عن دفئ يا خبنا
بهدوء إلى اللانهم تحت شفيقنا
نوم تصل يدغغ النجوم
أريد ... أنت ثاءب

أريد...أن أنام
حلماً لأن قائداً ما تحدث
تسمعني يا أمي
أراكم تمرحون بإطعام العطف ير
أراكم ضحك اللعب في أرجوحة الجنة
تشألوان ازقحية في نوم ملون
كزجاج تفتت تختلط الأحلام
يا أمي اقسم أني يته
لكن واحدٍ في غزة يحمل
أجرك الثلاث هداء
فبتت جهدا من كلمتق لاترى بالجراح
أريد ان اسمع من بضل الشمس
اقبض على بتلك الاسفنجة
التي أصبحت قتلية
هكذا منشين نحن على ريش
إلى أن نصل قمة التعب
وضع حلنا رونق لول
يا امي حي....غدا
سوف نحيا هنا.

So we don't sleep

I'm afraid to close my eyes,
O mother,
Your eyelash raises one question after another.
There's a story in your eyes—speak it.
Words yawn on my tongue,
They've lived there long enough.
Arise, O rubble,
Come out of me!
I no longer want to cradle you.
Perhaps I could breathe,
With a body freed from shrouds.
Send her out of our home.
Can we tidy the house one last time
Before we're displaced?
Can we photograph it for memory—
Store our laughter, our tears, our screams—
Then leave?
O sea stacked before us
Like a shy embrace
In a world not ours,
Can you send our echo to nearby oceans,
That a giant whale may strike the occupier's base?
Can we invent a new alphabet
For fear, for pain, for home,
So the world hears
That gray, continuous sound above us—
Buzzing planes,
Roaring rockets
Above green, above ruin,
Above a gravestone

Scrawled in charcoal on a burnt house,
The trace of a firebelt...
We won't tell them, "We said... and we said..."
A thousand times, the eyes sip from the sky
While we search for warmth
To gently carry us to sleep
Under our balcony,
A seamless sleep that tickles the stars.
I want... to yawn.
I want... to sleep.
I dreamed of some leader speaking—
Do you hear, mother?
I see you laughing, feeding the birds.
I see you playing on the swing of paradise,
Iridescent colors glowing in a rainbow slumber,
Like a bottle shaken—dreams all mixed inside.
O mother, I swear I saw it:
One shroud in Gaza holding
The bodies of three martyrs.
So I became a worn, wounded body
Groaning with pain.
I want to hear the heartbeat of the sun—
Or the heart itself... that sponge
Which has grown hard.
That's how we walk—on feathers—
Until we reach the peak of exhaustion
In full daylight, and say:
O Christ... tomorrow...
We shall live here.

ابتهاج

تغمرني اللحظة
ويهطل لحن الحياة
أسرّ النجوى و هيتساب؟
فيح خفي يغرّد ويطير
لطيور غناء يغرّدن متشريا
وهي تتدفق بين الحبين
فوق أغصان الغبطة
ثل شروق يتلألأ كهمسة
تحفّ بالحب، بالحياة
فيحمرّ تلألأى الغروب والرحيل
أصفرّ تو هج من ظلالي الشمس تضيء
جوال الصباح
وأخضرّ مغاب تلتشريين ها
خليج الكلام
تو ينسيها العليل
بفاج طفولتي.... وتورقن أثاي.

Joy

Overwhelmed by the present moment,
life's melody is awakening me.
Shall I capture this flowing melody?

A hidden joy that sings and flies away
Free and lost, chirping in ecstasy.
A sound that flows between lovers.

On the branches of joy
like a sunrise that steals in
like a whisper
Celebrating love.

In its redness, I forget the sunset, its farewell.
Its yellow glows from the sun's fragments
to illuminate the eyes of the morning.
And its green is a color of ecstatic forests.

The fluttering of words
Irrigates me with its sweet breeze.
It surprises my childhood
and makes me blossom
as a Woman.

كن حرًا

كن طائرا حرا
فلردجناحي روحك
لاتعها حبيسة قصص
خلف قضبان الثوابة.

من أعلق كتني على الأئلة
تشغي خيالء إلى ذهنك:
كيف يمكنني أن أغني مرة أخرى؟
من يرفع عني القيود؟
من يفتح لي الأبواب؟
هناك أشياء جيدة تخطك تاج الحياة،
ابحث عن سبيل حريتك
انطلق. و كن طائرا...وحلق.

حتى ترى خبايا أبعاد جيدة،
في دوظائر غامضة،
بعيدًا عن حياة تشحت بلار ماد
توثبت انتك
في ظلمة الليل،

وفي لحظة لا ترصدها الأعين،
حتى من جناح طائر في الهروب.

دع أعينك ترى النور،
هي تنمو وتشتبك في حر كة بداخلك،
تحرز للوجود.
أزح عن مكونك وطمأنين
أطلق عنانها
لطائر يحلق مثل ريشة تقف في السماء،
فيتلوا القيود عن رغبتك وتتعدد حجبتها.

Feel Free

Like the bird of your soul
Locked in the cage of everyday life
Behind the bars of coercion.

From the depths rises into your brain,
How can it sing again?
Who will give it freedom?
Who will open the bars?
New things urge you to try.
Find the way to freedom
and fly, fly, fly...

You want to explore other dimensions,
in unknown circles,
far away from the grey life
and prove yourself.

In the darkness of the night
in an unguarded moment
the bird could escape.

Show what is unexplored,
growing and stirring within you,
hidden for far too long
Cherished deep within.

Release it like a bird
that flies light as a feather in the sky,
so that your suppressed desire

may finally find its freedom.

ولَنْ تَتَغادر
في غرفةٍ ثمّ من قناديل الصوتُ "بلقَ"
بيتٌ للعنكبوت
في الزاويةِ التي في شمال الشمال
لم تزحزحْهُ الريح.
بيتٌ لسُوديم غرفتك
تُبقي لَتخْمْ في طبع رسلة
رُدَّت لِصاحبها لَمْ مِفْتَحْ.
لتبهتَ من محتِ للبصمات
وغارَ الأيّامَ عن الانتظارة
بقطعة من خِمار جدّتك،
وأزحت سِتارةً من الغصون والأوراق.
موحلاً لا يزالُ طريقُك للضريح
لا يلذّ لك البرد
لولا هذه الأيّام، قلتَ،
ما جهدي لتي يريك ها البريع
إلاّ سحابة هطلتْ فيَّ وحدي
وتتلونتلك للّه
من فستقيّ يفرفُ في قبر جدّي

إلى السماوي في عيني ابنتي

While leaving

While leaving a Sunny Room
A Voice called saying:"Stay"
The Spider's house
In the right Angle of the northern window
Has not been touched by the wind
A black house imprinted
on your window like traces
Of a seal on the stamp of a letter
Returned unopened to the sender
You noticed it
When you cleansed your eyeglasses
of fingerprints& the dust of days
With a piece of your grandmother's headscarf,
And pulled back a curtain
of branches and leaves:
Your narrow road still is muddy.
You do not savor the cold.
Were it not for these days, you said,
My life that's been confused by spring
Would be a cloud that rained only on me
And changed the colors of that hill:
From pistachio-green fluttering above
my grandfather's grave
To the sky-blue of my daughter's eyes.

Oladele Babajamu (Nigeria): Poem in Yoruba

ÀSẸ̀ OGUN KORÒ

Ìpèsè ogun korò
Àṣe ogun kan
Èdè àiyèdè ló ń bí ogun
Àwọn olọtẹ̀ a wí pé
Bó le dìjà kó dìjà
Bó lè dogun kó do ogun
Tó bá di ogun tán
A sì dì ọ̀rọ̀ sùnùkùn
Bẹ̀ẹ̀ni ọ̀rọ̀ sùnùkùn
Ojú sùnùkùn la fi ń wò ó

Àṣẹ̀ ogun korò
Àwọn olósẹ̀lú á dáa sílẹ̀
Àwọn olojẹ̀lú á ṣe ìpèṣẹ̀
Àwọn ológun ní sì má ń jẹ
Àti àwọn ará ìlú
Tí kò mọwó tábí mẹsẹ̀
Tí wọn bá sì jẹun tán
Á di májèlë ikú
Àwọn tí ikú kò bá sì pa
Wọn á di rádaràda
Tàbí aláàbọ̀ ara
Àwọn mìíràn a sì wà nínú ipò
Agbede méjì ayé àti ọ̀run

Àwọn ọmọ ológun tórí bá kó yọ
Wọn á di akọni àtẹni iyì
Nítorí pé àtàrí Àjànàkú kìí ṣẹ ẹrù ọmọdé

Pẹ̀lú ìrora àtìrọjú
lábẹ aṣọ àìkinba ìkógun ti wọn
Tí wón fara káásá
Nígbà tí wón fi ojú wi iná
Ninu gbigbona ogun

WAR IS A BITTER DISH

War is bitterness
War is a result of conflict
When parties settled for war
And allows gun to speak rather
Than the mouth
The issue of war is a complex one
Which must be accurately deliberated on
The feast of war is bitter
Politicians kick start the process
Business men enjoy the provision
Served to eat the intestines
Of the warrior and the innocents
Makes life useless
Makes no sense
From the senselessness
Of a war
Are unconscious souls
Empty body cases
And dead men walking

War consumes the purpose of living
Annihilate visions and dreams
Leaving behind scars too deep
And difficult to erase
Yet bequeathing memories for living veteran
Who shine with stars and medals
Of victory adorned with hidden scars
Beneath their war garment.

Wafula Khisa (Kenya): Poems in Lubukusu (a dialect of Luhya language)

Basecha Bano

Basecha bano boma kimioyo, wakhalila sabesindukha tawe
Bakhulaka likulu wauka oli olichayo
Nono bakhulekha wora kumumu, nawikalangasia amuliango
Nibo bakenda enje khulisia chimoni na khulia bulai
Basecha bano kang'ali sabakhuchumila tawe.

Ewe nawisinga ne chindemu muluchi, nibo bacha muhot shower
Ewe nokona enjala buli endalo, nibo bacha five-star for supper
Ewe nawisilikha ne kamanyasi, nibo bacha India, special treatment
Ewe nokonela kamasafu nga enduyu, nibo balia chipizza ne chisausage
Basecha bano kang'ali sabakhuchumila tawe.

Basecha bano babalaa chinda, bakhefunda sisiaki sabekura tawe
Nabanyola likumba balomanga bali linda, bakhupangile kimilimo na kimiandu bakhuwe
Nono ewe nosilinda bikwe wangale, okhatikhe kamakia nowenja bufu
Okhape sibi nokhong'onda kimiliango, noenja limotole wome chimbafu nga bakofu
Balebe lelo nawenya buyeti okhoya okhumanyile
Basecha bano kang'ali sabakhuchumila tawe.

Basecha bano basima bichwisi, mali safi bikhalimo kamapala tawe
Biechiskati chinyimbi nga kimishipi, bibarusianga lukesi
Biechislit chindeyi nga engila echa paradiso, bikilanga bachukha kamare kawe
Biabesunga mumabeka nga bibambilwe khumusalapa, bienja salvation
Babirusie khumutambo na khubispoila na kimiandu
Batumbula chisebele chosi wanywamo luweni lukhupa!
Basecha bano bakhubasa bikele, wandase solinyola busime nokhalimo sindu tawe.

Ewe wanala khubafumia naupa chimbi, manya oli enje embi
Ewe wanala khubatimila nobasikamila, lelo wakwa khurumikha nga engila
Nabacha mucanaan bakhumwata nga sitasi, khubela otamba limanya ne kamakesi
Basecha bano basima esilingi, wabebasamo luweni lukhupa
Basecha bano kang'ali sabakhuchumila tawe.

These Men

These men are cruel; they are never moved by your tears
They promised you paradise and you thought they'd deliver
Now they've left you in scorching sun, doing nothing for yourself
As they tour the world, eating and drinking fine things
These men really don't work for us.

As you bathe in snake-infested rivers, they take hot showers
As you sleep hungry every day, they dine and wine in five-star hotels
As you cure yourself with herbs, they seek special treatment in India
As you eat leaves like a rabbit, they enjoy pizza and sausages
These men really don't work for us.

These men are greedy, they're never satisfied even if they swallow a granary
When they get power, they always tell you to wait for them to create jobs for you
As you wait for them to fulfil promises, you'll starve and suffer
You'll get tired of knocking on people's doors, begging for money
You won't get help if you lack connections these days
These men really don't work for us.

These men love beautiful girls
Those that wear miniskirts turn them on
Those that wear dresses with long slits make them to salivate

They hang on their shoulders as if they're on the cross, thirsting for salvation
To be saved from poverty and spoiled with cash
These men have contaminated all rivers, you'll be struck by lightning if you drink from them
They've ruined everything, you won't find love without money, brother.

As you praise and clap for them, you must know how terrible things are
To them you're merely a path to their destination
They'll abandon you like a rag once they get there because you're a fool
These men love money, they'll crash you if you challenge them
These men really don't work for us.

Nanjala Wange

Okhakhusima kang'ali okhupia sibi mwana wa mai
Ese nechubile sonyakhana nendi omulamu
Nyala nakhwalila lulimi okendelekho wiulile bulai
Nga oli musinyifu naulilanga nosambwa na kumumu.

Nyala nakhufulila lisiati wibimbe nga linyenya efula nekwa
Okhatora tawe, walwala ufuniakaka kumoyo kwebena
Kheme imara nga lisisi lia Berlin, sisiafusie sikhakhuucha wakwa
Khubela ewe watikia likulu, nawisisikha limenya liange likarangarana.

Esese nyala nakonela kamare nasibombile olie wikure
Khubela ewe kumoyo kwange, nokikona ese chilia
Ewewe etala yange, babekomba osime bakhalinde sire
Efwe khusimane enyanga ekwe nga Romeo nende Julia.

Nono nembolanga endi efwe khwamile atayi
Bakhamanyile tawe bauka bali khwasimanila mufour
Baliyo bembiya chinganakani, nababona khufwana bulayi
Bauka bali biakwile khwangala, nyo khuambane nga sitaki nengubo.

Nanjala esese simanga wele kakhuumba obe owange
Bindu nabindumile ewe otikiya limenya liange
Abanga busime bakusia nga chinyanya lelo
Andi sili omusumba, nibasa bikele nyo ngone lilo.

Ewe wekana basecha bechisuti, bali na kimiandu nga bunyalu
Wanjiyama nekhali na sindu, nekhali kamaroro kelikulu
Ewe wekana bibitina na sileka, bionaka enju bandu bapa sibi
Khubela lukoba lufumila omukhasi, nokona enjala bubi.

Nono mwana wa mai khusaba sindu silala
Sibala nasibiya khukhoya khweumba alala khukhalekhana
Khuyetane nga sitaki nengubo khubimbe sichula
Na khuluma kumoyo nga eswa mwiloba nakhunyalana.

Nanjala My Love

He who doesn't love you can really cause you pain
And I swear I won't let you suffer while I'm still alive
I can spread my tongue on the ground for you to walk on & feel good
Like he who stands in a shade while you're scorched by the sun.

I can remove my shirt for you to cover yourself like an umbrella when it rains
You shouldn't be rained on; you may fall sick & break my heart to bleed
I'll stand firm like the Berlin Wall, to hold you not be blown away by strong winds
Because you hold the sky, if you shake my life will fall apart.

I can sleep on an empty stomach as long as yours is full
Because you are my heart, it'll hurt me if you sleep hungry
You are my light, those who wish you go off will wait in vain
Let's love each other until sunset, like Romeo and Juliet.

So when I say that we've come from far
Those who don't understand think we fell in love in class four
There are those with warped minds who see us looking pretty
And think we got everything on a silver platter before we stuck together like a button & a cloth.

Nanjala, I always thank God for creating you to be mine
When things get hard, it's you who holds my life
If love was sold like tomatoes today
I'd still be a bachelor, sleeping with a hand between my legs.

I'm glad you rejected classy men with immense wealth like dirt
And took me in, a man with nothing except colourful dreams
I'm glad you rejected gossiping & rudeness, they break homes & cause suffering
Because home is praised because of a woman, it's bad when you starve.

So, daughter of my mother, I beseech you
If the world comes to its knees, let's stick together
Help each other like a button & a cloth to cover our nakedness
And be strong and forgiving in case we hurt each other.

Sumba Kienyuma

Waulile likulu liakukume, kamame akosi kanjile
Notamba likabuti wiyikame namwe linyenya okule
Babola mbo mbayo okhalame, efula naicha yamabale
Siliyo obira keyame, butinyu nabwichile
Babesaya mbo mwirume, khutimanie omusiku khale
Mwaleka mbo chingacho, mwamuwa endebe kekhale
Efwe sumba kienyuma khakhupe sibi nono.

Bamubolela mbo mwichunge, naburobora babami
Namusima mwikane bechinge, babanulanula chinimi
Namunyala mwikane babefwi, bakhamwibile kamaroro
Mukhoya mwekana bakhalukha, bakhakile kumutambo kumwire
Belebe mwekala kamaru, mwatimila bitasi
Nono khamwilocha sina embeo, chisusi nachiluma?
Efwe sumba kienyuma khakhupe sibi nono.

Nono khamulila sina, nabamuswena mwikonjo?
Burafu bwakhakila mwebena, manya mbo kamenaka kionjo
Mwasamilila kimwinwa na mukikona, namwinyokha chinju batechule
Mwatabukhe chilong'i lelo, namwitikhula khurunga kamakobi
Mwasangalila bibiuma biefwe nabakusia, khubela mwasima khulia bimali
Muchuli enje neluma, balebe mukhalie wananu?
Efwe sumba kienyuma khakhupe sibi nono.

Wretched Men

You've heard the sky roaring; you can see it's started drizzling
You should find a shade if you've no jacket or buy an umbrella
They said nobody will survive when hailstorms and thunderstorms come
They pleaded with us not to relent when chasing evil out of our home
But you ignored, thinking they were mere stories & embraced it
Let's pay now, we wretched men.

They told you to be careful when electing leaders
To reject the stingy that come with sugary tongues
To reject the thieves that would steal your dreams
To reject the greedy that would make poverty kill you
But you chose not to listen and fell for these rags
Now why are you complaining of the cold & bedbugs when they bite?
Let's pay now, we wretched men.

Why are you crying now when they step on your wounds?
Even if you bleed from pain, know it's just the beginning
You'll sleep hungry and wake up to find your house torn apart
You'll soon wear rags as you bleed to pay endless debts
You celebrated privatization of our industries, for you're used to eating droppings
When things go south soon, from whose plate will you eat?
Let's pay now, we wretched men.

Jabulani Mzinyathi (Zimbabwe): Poems in chiShona)

Ndosvoda

Kugona yedu mitauro
Chakava chiseko
Takamera zenze
Dzevamwe ndimi tosvisvina
Ndogara ndozvidya moyo

Ko, idzo mhidigari dzechiRungu
Vanondinzwisisa vamwe vangu vangani
Ndototsvakawo muturikiri
Muturikiri wokutaura neverudzi rwangu
Kana uya asina kana kusimira
Kusvoda ndotomudarika ini

Ashamed

Mastering our languages
That brought ridicule
Started the bragging
Embracing foreign languages
My mind now in turmoil

Linguistic gymnastics in English
Understood by few of my people
Needing the services of an interpreter
Failing to reach out to my people
Even a nude person has lesser shame

Afrika

Afrika
misodzi
dikita
ropa
marangwanda

Rinopisa sadza
Wakariguma rini Afrika

Wakaritakudzwa resimbi jogwe
Ndiwe wakatadzei Afrika

Vako vanopedzwa vana
Hwako upfumi vevamwe vachichapfanya

Simukazve Afrika
Kuve nhapwa ramba zvachose

Africa

Africa
Tears
Sweat
Blood
Time whitened bones

When was the last time
The last time you had peace

You were made to carry a steel yoke
What sin did you commit, Africa

Your children annihilated
Your wealth enjoyed elsewhere

Arise Africa
Cast off shackles and chains

Zvedu

Nguva hatichina
Nguva yokutambisa
Yokupedza udzvanyiriri
Ndiyo yoga yasara
Yokuzvinzwira tsitsi hatina
Utema uhwu hwamunoona
Kwete hausi hurwere
Tinotodada nahwo
Akasarudza ruvara rweganda rake hapana
NaNyadenga tose takapiwa
Yedu mitauro yakapfumawo imi
Teererai munzwe mitakunanzva
Dzedu tsika hadzisemesi
Tega tinoziva zvakanaka nezvakaipa
Dzakatesvera njere tinadzo
Vedu vanachiremba tinodada navo
Nyangwe movanyomba sei
Hatisi rudzi rwekudurunhuru

Inheritance

No time to waste
Time to end oppression
To end all subjugation
That is all in sight
No time for self pity
This dark skin you see
That is not an ailment
Proud of this melanin
Not one chose their skin colour
Our maker gave each one that
Our languages have opulence
Listen to the sweetness
Our ways are not putrid
We can tell right from wrong
That we never learnt from others
Keen minds we have in abundance
We have pride in our traditional doctors
Those you derisively call witch doctors
We are not a dung heap people

Dzidziso Dzavo

Takadzikabira dzidziso
Dzidziso dzeupenzi

Inzwai zvavakatidzidzisa
Vaitodyara tsangadzi mune yedu minda

Wapiwa ganyamuto padama
Gamuchira nemufaro wopa rimwe dama

Kana ukadzipurwa ziso
Chitobvuma rimwe ritiburwe

Mbeu yeshoko iri ndokudzika midzi
Nhai mhai zvahuri upenzizve

Chiteerera kwazvakazoguma
Watorerwa bindu, rega nyika yose vatore

Their Teachings

Swallowed hook, line and sinker
Lessons brought by knaves

Listen to what they taught
Sowing weeds in our fields

Given a thunderous slap
Turn the other cheek in submission

If one eye is plucked out
Allow them to gouge out the other

The tiny seed became a tree
Lunacy took root

The final show down came
When they take your field
Let them have the whole country

Mapfupa Achamuka

Mutsipa usati watyorwa
Mutengesi asati abvuta gonan'ombe
Mbuya vakataura
'Angu Mapfupa achamuka'

Hope takavashaisa
Uyu waive wabvira moto

Chakava Chimurenga
Teererai unzwe mwana wevhu

Mapfupa achamukazve
Ngozi muchaiona imi vatengesi

Teereresai riya izwi
'Angu Mapfupa achamuka!'

Bones Will Rise

Before her neck was broken
The turncoat had not taken the snuff box
Had not taken her protective snuff box.
That spirit medium declared
'My bones will rise!'

Sleepless nights we gave them
That fire was blazing

That was the liberation struggle
Child of the soil listen

Those bones will rise again
An avenging spirit against traitors

Listen and fully understand
'My bones will rise!'

Jalaludeen Ibrahim (Nigeria): Poems in Hausa

A DAREN YAU

Gong! Gong! Gong!
Sautin shela yana amo,
Kamar kira mai ƙarfi,
Sautin na ratsa dare,
Kowane lungu da saƙon gari.

Ga mai shela ya fito,
Domin isar da muhimmin sako,
Sarauniya bata bayyana ba.
Fadar Sarki ta shiga ruɗani.
Shelar yau saƙon Maimartaba ce.

Gong! Gong! Gong!
Sautin shela yana ƙara amo,
Yana ƙara kutsawa lungu da saƙo,
Neman nasarar bayyanar Sarauniya.
Oh, Sarauniya ina kika ɓoye,
Fadar Sarki na cikin juyayi.
Sarki ya kasa zama ya kasa tsayi,
Har sai Sarki yaga bayyanar Sarauniya,
Cikin koshin lafiya da ƙasaita irin ta sarauta.

TONIGHT

Gong! Gong! Gong!
The sounds echo loudly,
Through the stillness,
Like a clarion call,
Piercing the midnight air.

I am the village town crier,
Announcing a sacred mission.
The Queen has yet to return home,
And the Palace is on edge.
Here, I carry forth the king's message,
Brimming with hope and longing.

Gong! Gong! Gong!
These echoes travel to the next village,
In search of the missing Queen.
Oh, Melanin Queen, hear my call.
The Palace stands in silence.
The King is resolute yet restless,
Aching to hear the bells of your footsteps.

SARAUNIYA KYAKKYAWA

Ga Sarauniya,
Ainihin jarumar Afirka.
Launin fatarta mai kyawon asali
Siffarta tamkar zinariya,
Kyakkyawa abun ban sha'awa.

Hasken idanuwanta kamar lu'ulu'u
Kalar leɓanta kyakkyawa abun burgewa,
Dogon hanci kamar larabawan asali,
Ƙamshinta tamkar furen róz,
Ga murmushi mai ratsa jiki.

Sarauniya mai baiwa da basira,
Daga ke ba sauran wata bukata.
Kece farin cikin rayuwata.
Nayi sa'a da samun masoyiya tamkar ki.

Garin masoyi baya nisa.
Daga birnin Maradun har Sin,
Duk inda kike zan same ki,
Domin jaddada maki soyayya ta.

Sarauniyata abun alfararina,
Na baki amanar so masoyiyata,
Ƙaunarki ta mamaye zuciya ta,
Kin zamo tamkar bugun zuciya a gare ni.

MELANIN QUEEN

Behold, I present
The Melanin Queen,
A true African heroine.
Chocolate, olive skin.
This light-tanned tone
Yes, Melanin is powerful.

Like diamonds, her eyes glitter.
Her lips, the purple apples,
Succulent and flourishing.
Her nose, the fragrance of a rose,
Her charming smile, a warm hello.

She is a poetess to admire;
She is that morning dew,
Each droplet is so gentle and mild,
A reflection of a new dawn.
What more could I seek,
Than this Melanin Beauty?

Beyond the walls of Maradun
A white rose blooms
Like the morning-glory
Fleeting subtle fragrance
And these twining vines
Ascend the trellises of my soul

The purity of the white rose
Envelopes my very being
From the wake of dawn

Until dusk brews quietly.
This recurring feeling
A message of the heartbeat.

Bonface Nyamweya (Kenya): Poems in Ekegusii

Ekeng'entambori

Emee! Yasibire aiga, rora, etomberete
Eyeng'enta? Eyang'entwa? Eyarukunywa?
Mbare baiteire chindende baegwe rini
Mbare bachire bichuko, mbaunenkigwa
Chinkoro amagicho chiaberorokire na koerera
Enkoro etaberoroke, yaitereire
Ogochana tasoncha chiono ne'chiosi chiechiro
Ere n'eono n'eosi etari 'chiro
Ekiagera oboono n'oboosi mbore mbwa
Chiekeng'entambori gotukorigwa na gotukoreka
Bing'entambori mbiri kiambori
Bing'entambori mbiri kong'enta mbori
Embori nao ekweng'entera
Ekebichori egetabigu, gioka nkeng'ente embori?
'Kebichori getabichoka gekundo, giaitire embori!
Inee ning'o rende ekeng'entambori?
Kiang'entang'entire chimee chitari'inke
Korende eromberere ye'chimee
Nigo ekweng'entera aroro
Ase ogweetanania aroro. Ase ogwekundekera aroro
Eenchebano. Eombogano. Esisikano. Ekwerekererano.
Obotati bwembori eye bwaenekirie iga:
Embori, n'ekeng'entambori
Obombori, n'ekeng'entambori
Chiamate chiembori, n'ekeng'entambori
Omosibi n'omosibori mbori, n'ekeng'entambori
Egesiberambori, n'ekeng'entambori
Egeitambori, n'ekeng'entambori

Mborie, komanyete nkeng'entambori ki kere ekeng'entambori?

The Forget Me Not

The goat that was tied here, look, it's dead
Did it strangle itself? Was it strangled? Was it hit?
Some have salivated to be given the liver
Others have run away, not to be interrogated
Thousands of hearts have been shocked
A heart that won't be shocked, has assumed
Who runs away not to see the rude and mad of the market
Is a rude and mad without a market
Because rudeness and madness have habits
Of a forget me not to be probed
The forget me nots are docile
The forget me nots do not strangle a goat
It is where a goat strangles itself
A loose loop, will it alone strangle a goat?
The inexorable knot has strangled a goat
So, who is the forget me not?
The forget me not has strangled many goats
But several of these goats
Strangle themselves at the forget me not
By rotating themselves there. By fixing themselves there.
Aimless. Pointless. Fixation. Insistence.
An investigation of this goat has revealed:
A goat is a forget me not
Goatness is a forget me not
Neighbours of a goat are a forget me not
The tier and loosener of a goat are a forget me not
The rope is a forget me not
The killer of a goat is a forget me not
Let me ask, do you know which forget me not is the forget me not?

UKULUNGA LOKUQONDISWA.

Olungileyo nguye olungisisayo,
Olungisiswayo usol' umlungisi.
Umlungis' ulangazelel' ukulungiswa.
Kanti kulungel' abanjani?
Abangani babosilungile sebekulungele
konk' okulungileyo lokubafaneloyo.
Imfanelo, yisiph' esifanel' olungileyo,
um' eselungisil' iziqondiso wanqoba.
Phela kunqotshwa okubi lobubi.

Ububi, abubuqondis' ububi.
Ububi, bemb' amathun' angela mkhawulo.
Ububi, ngobubi bengez' ubuth' emhlabeni.
Bona bubi, mbangela yobumpumputh' emhlabeni.
Ababi kumele balungisiswe kulunge,
Baqondis' izenzo bagiye ngokulunga.
Banganqekuza bayikhothamel' imfundiso yobuhle lokulungileyo.

Lumhlaba phel' onakele,
Uding' ukuhlanzwa, ugezwe, uqondiswe.
Phel' ukuqond' akusikuba msulwa,
Ukuqonda yimizamo yobuhle bokulunga,
Umhlaba ngokwayo kumel' ubeyingxenye yokuqonda.
Uqonde nta okukaSolobhoni ngimqonda.
Abalungileyo labo baqhubeke kundlelanhle yokuqondisisa...

Explanation

The poem highlights the urgent need for humanity to reflect

and rethink its path. It calls for a return to the original purpose of creation and a renewal of our commitment to serve and protect one another from the cruelty of the modern world. It emphasizes that unity of purpose, collective effort, and speaking with one voice are vital to building a renewed and better life. At its core, the poem is a plea for peace, love and unity, values that are essential for healing both people and the planet. It reminds us that no lasting change can happen in isolation, and that only through compassion and solidarity can we rise above the chaos. The world is in need of a collective awakening, a conscious return to the sacred bond that once connected all living beings.

Ngcali Angelica Xhegwana (South Africa): Poems in isiXhosa

Iimvakalelo

Awukhe ubiwe bubuzaza bamehlo omntu
ohleli ecaleni kwakho, iingqimba zomkhence
zinyibilika ezandleni zakho, amaza ebetheka
kwiziqhitsi zamanye, esenza ingoma emyoli
kwiindlebe zakho ezivingcwe bubu mdaka?

Awukhe ujule amehlo akho phezulu ubone
ukukhanya okugqamileyo kweenkwenkwezi
ezizalelwe phezu kwezibhakabhaka ezicocekileyo
zasebusuku? Ingaba ngamanye amathuba
amehlo akho akakhe alunguze na
kwizibhakabhaka ezingenasiphelo ube nemibuzo
engapheliyo? Ingaba awukhe ukhwanqiswe
kusini na bubume belizwe obunjengephupha?
Ewe, ilizwe likhangeleka
ngathi lingumdlalo, sonke sileqa
umgca okrweliweyo osisiphelo.
Singaqondi ukuba bekungekho
mdyarho kwasekuqaleni, suke
sonke sisutywe kukufa phakathi
endleleni. Ngamanye amathuba

awukhe uphakamise umnwe wakho
uwujikelezise emoyeni, ungakholwa
kukubona imimangaliso enokwenziwa
yingqondo yakho? Awukhe ngamanye

amathuba ucinge ungakholwa
ngumsebenzi onokwenziwa
ngumlinganiselo omnye womphefumlo
emzimbeni wakho?

Senses

Have you ever been stolen by the seriousness of someone's eyes
sitting next to you, thick ice
melting in your hands, waves beating
against rocks, making beautiful music
to your ears that are blocked by dirt?

Did you ever turn your eyes up to look at the shining
bright starts that were formed
in the clean skies
of the night? Do your eyes sometimes
ponder over
the endless skies and have endless
questions? Are you ever shocked
by the dreamy appearance of the earth?
Yes, the world looks like a game, and we are all chasing
an endless line.
Not aware that there was
no race to begin with,
then death catches us on
the way. At other times

do you ever lift your finger
and wave it in the air, and not believe
the miracles that
your brain can perform? Do you ever
sometimes believe what one breath
in your body can do?

Translated from isiXhosa by Mantoa Motinyane

Inqugwala elingcwele

Apho kukho iintambiso ezizukileyo namachiza
Apho phezu komhlaba kuhlala iintsimbi ezisasaziweyo
   ne mizi
Apho amakhukho neengqayi zomdongwe zifihlwe khona
Apho imilenze ediniweyo enemivambo iphumla khona
Apho ubulumko bakwaNtu buphakulwa khona
   ziinkonde neenkondekazi
Apho amantombanzanana afunda ukuqingqa iimbiza
Apho abafana abancinci bagwencela baya ebudodeni
Apho kuthathwa khona izigqibo
Apho ubuxoki nemfihlo zizinyeliswa khona
Apho abantwana babamba iimpefumlo zabo
   zatanci
Apho abadala bathatha iimpefumlo zabo
   zokugqibela

The sacred old hut

Where lies sacred lotions and potions
Where on the ground stays scattered beads
and reeds
Where grass mats and clay pots are hidden
Where tired wrinkled feet come to rest
Where legends are told by elders
Where young girls learn to make pots
Where young boys turn into men
Where decisions are made
Where lies and secrets are kept
Where children take their first breaths
Where the old take their last
Right there, in the sacred old hut.

David Chasumba (Zimbabwe): Poems in chiShona

Handina kuvinga sadza pamusha pano

Ndati tiyeuchidzane baba vevana
Kuti handina kuvinga sadza pamusha pano
Kumba kwedu sadza raiveko
Randaimona gobvu rinenge dete
Ndakavinga rudo rwenyu pamusha pano, Mbano, Matemai

Wakaidzidza kupiko, iyo tsika yekubva kubasa
Uchisvikira kubhawa, usati wandiswedza nevana?
Haunyare here, murume mukuru,
Kudzadzarika kunge mbuyamuderere,
Pakati peusiku wakananga kumba?
Uchipinda mumba kunge muroyi
Wondimutsa kuti ndidziyise sadza ratonhora
Inga makagarika Matemai
Inga makakupuka Mbano
Roora renyu ririkushanda kwazvo!

Kasadza kacho munonyobvora nyobvora
Kunge kanosemesa, mapindwa neiko nhai baba vevana?
Muri kubikwirwa kupiko, nhai Matemai?
Makadyiswa mupfuhwira upiko, nhai Mbano?

Zvepabonde handichataura, murume mukuru,
Kurukutika, nekuchimbidza basa kunge jongwe
Ndati tiyeuchidzane baba vevana
Kuti handina kuvinga sadza pamusha pano
Rudo rwenyu ndiro rakandikwezva Matemai
Parwai kwata kunge sadza riripamoto.

Mati ndogara ndega here seshirikadzi,
Imi muripo, zvamavakutaura zvekuenda
Kumarimuka, kuJoni?
Munoda kuti ndisare ndichiriritira vana ndirindega here
Nekutengesa madomasi pamusika
Imi muchinosasana zvenyu ikoko kuJobheki
Inga zvakanzi *kusasana kunoparira wani*?

Rudo rwenyu rwapwa semvura yepazambuko
Chibudai pachena, Matemai, mondipawo gupuro
Handina kusiya ndapisa musha wevabereki vangu
Ndinyareiwo murume wangu

Ndiri kutapudza chigumbu
Chiri muninga yemoyo wangu
Ndati tiyeuchidzane Mbano
Kuti handina kuvinga sadza pamusha pano
Ndakavinga rudo rwenyu, Matemai

I Did Not Come for Sadza at This Homestead

May I remind you, my dear husband, Matemai,
That I didn't marry you for food
There was plenty of *Sadza* at my parents' home,
I married you for love

Where did you learn such unloving behaviour
Of clocking off work and heading off straight
To the pub before serenading me and the kids?
Where did you learn such unloving behavior
Of staggering home at midnight like a drunken mantis
Bursting into our house like a witch
And demanding that I wake up to warm your food
Oh, you blessed cow!
Did you pay the bride price to live like a king
And use me, like your Downtown Abbey servant?

You eat a morsel of *Sadza*
Like my food is poisoned or stale
What is the matter, my husband, Matemai
Is someone feeding you, my love?
Is someone giving you a love portion, my love?

I won't even dare talk about lovemaking
You lost the sparks in bed
You jump on and off the trampoline
And get it over with
In seconds, like a rooster

Shall I now live like a widow
When you plan to emigrate to greener pastures

In Johannesburg, South Africa, in search of work
How will I fend for the kids alone
With meagre income from selling vegetables
At the marketplace?
You will reap what you sow
If you pleasure other women
While neglecting your family

If our love is over, say so
Give a token to show that our love is over
I didn't burn down my parents' home,
Please show me some love and respect, my husband.

This is my lamentation
From the cave of my grieving heart
Let me remind you, my love
That I didn't marry you for the food
There was plenty of *Sadza* at my parents' home
I married you for deep love
I beseech you, my husband, reciprocate my love

Regai ndinyarare hangu

Kana matsotsi ochengetedza dura
Kana makonzo otambira mudura
Regai ndinyarare hangu

Kana munhu akafuma yavambinga
Pasina ziya kana mabhindauko
Regai ndinyarare hangu

Kana vabvakure vava kuchera
Zvicherwa zvenyika yedu vokutengesa kumhiri
Regai ndinyarare hangu

Kana tikapedza mombe mudanga
Asi dhighiri racho roshaya basa
Regai ndinyarare hangu

Kana vane mari voenda kumhiri
Kunorapwa kuzvipatara zveko
Regai ndinyarare hangu

Kana shoroma dzoendesa vana
Kuzvikoro kune dzimwe nyika
Regai ndinyarare zvangu

Kana vanhu vazhinji vave maporofita
Anoporofita kune vanotambura
Regai ndinyarare hangu

Kana vana vedu vopengeswa nemutoriro
Pasina asungirwa kutengesa mutoriro

Regai ndinyarare hangu

Kana vanasikana vofamba vakashama
Manheru kukwezva varume
Regai ndinyarare hangu

Kana sabhuku vavondonga musha
Varume vakati tende, vakadzi vachipururudza
Regai ndinyarare zvangu

Kana vana votiza misha
Kunotsvaga raramo kumisha yemhiri
Regai ndinyarare hangu

Kana mapurisa avane huwori
Hwekukoronyera vatyairi mumigwagwa
Regai ndinyarare hangu

Kana vakashata vopunyuka jeri
Vasina nhaka vorambira mutorongo
Regai ndinyarare hangu

Mungazoti nyanduri vadhakwa neChibuku
Kunge Silas Mavende akaimbwa naSaintfloew
Saka regai ndinyarare hangu

My lips will be sealed

When the corrupt hold the keys
To the nations' treasury
My lips will be sealed

When someone becomes a tycoon
Overnight without breaking sweat
My lips will be sealed

When foreign businesses mine
And loot our nation's precious minerals
My lips will be sealed

When we sell all the livestock
But our children earn worthless degrees
My lips will be sealed

When someone becomes a prophet
Prophesying to the poor people only
My lips will be sealed

When the rich send their kids
To study in universities abroad
My lips will be sealed

When the rich seek treatment abroad
And not in local hospitals
My lips will be sealed

When our children are drug addicted
And no one is arrested for drug trafficking

My lips will be sealed

When the girlchild sells her body
I will be too hurt to talk
My lips will be sealed

When corrupt police officers
Mane the road blocks
My lips will be sealed

When the headman is incompetent
But the men nod, and women ululate
My lips will be sealed

When people abandon our village
Searching for greener pastures in distant villages
My lips will be sealed

When the innocent languishes in prison
But the guilty walks free
My lips will be sealed

Though my lips are sealed
Seeing such social injustices
My verse is my megaphone

Ndipembedzewo mudzimai wangu

Musi wandinochimbidza kusvika kumba
Ndisina kumira mira kubhawa
Ndisina kunwira nwira navanaMaidei
Ndipembedzewo mudzimai wangu

Pandinokutengera nhumbi dzakanaka
Nezvihwitsi zvevana zvinonaka
Ndipembedzewo mudzimai wangu, Sekai,
Kuti zvigare zvakadaro Mbano Matemai

Pandinotambira kupera kwemwedzi
Ndipembedzewo mudzimai wangu, Sekai,
Wonditenda nemutupo kuti, 'Zvaitwa Mbano, Matemai,
Chikwaka, VeGoromonzi, Chiuya chinenge mukaka,
chinodyiwa nevasina meno.'

Paruzhinji ndipembedzewo mudzimai wangu, Sekai,
Kuti ndinyemwerere nekuzvitutumadza
Paunoti 'Matemai vanondipa rudo rwunodakadza.'

Kana ukandipembedza mudzimai wangu
Kana mhembwe ndinomhanyisa ndikaibata
Ndigokupa mudzimai wangu
Nekuti murume munhu
Anotodawo kupembedzwa kuti amere zenze.

Compliment me, my love

When I arrive home
Straight from work
And didn't stop by the pub
And drink one for the road
Nor hang around the pretty pub virgins
Complement me, my love

When I buy you a lovely dress
And goodies for the children
Sing praises for me
That I may continue to shower you with presents

When I bring home the bacon
Sing me the old praise song
The totem praise song,
'Hail, the generous one, the unblemished one,
The one like lifesaving milk for the toothless one.'

Complement me in public, my love
Praise me to the stratosphere
Show me affection in public
That all women may envy you
For marrying the man of your dreams

Complement me, my love
A man needs love like a family pet
His big ego needs constant massaging.

Mhodzi yamakadyara: Rangariro

Kuti tiwane maguta
Kuti tirove nzara nembama
Maishanda nesimba, Amai
Kubata jongwe nemuromo
Kunodyara chibage nekukavira nzungu nenyimo
Ivhu rizere dova, zuva risati rarova nhongonya

Mai, maive shirikadzi inenjere
Shirikadzi hurudza, yaitarisa mwaka yegore
Nekunamata kuti dai denga
Radiridza minda yenyu nemisodzi yayo
Kuti tiwane chikafu

Mai, mhodzi yamakadyara
Mandiri, mupfungwa dzangu
Mhodzi yekushanda nesimba
Yakazobereka mhodzi iya
Ndinokutendai zvikuru, amai
Kuti hakunazve vamwe mai semi
Makandidzidzisa hunhu wakanaka
Makandidzidzisa kusakura kwakanaka
Makandidzidzisa kukohwa pakuru

Kunyangwe makazondisiya nerufu
Iyi irangariro yangu, mai, yekutenda
Kuti bhanzi ramakabika ravakudyika
Kuti muti wamakadyara wazokura
Wavakubereka mango dzinotapira samare

The Seeds That Bore Fruit (in memorium)

That your family could thrive
And live without strife
You woke up at cock crow
Your task was to hoe
The dew-soaked fields
Before sunrise and dusk
You were a widow
With a farmer's faith and patience
Who sowed good seeds
In the fertile soil
In due season
And prayed for the heavens
To water your back-breaking toil
Mother, you planted good seeds
Of hard work and determination
In the furrows of my mind
Mother, you were one of a kind
Who taught me about good deeds
Who taught me to uproot weeds
Who taught me to harvest good yields
Though you never lived stronger
Though you never lived longer
To witness the harvest in me
This poem is for you;
Thank you for baking me
Your son is now a cooked bun,
Thank you for planting
Good seeds that took root
Thank you for the nurturing done

Your son is a ripe mango tree
That bears succulent fruit.

N.B: This poem by David Chasumba was first published in Issue 6, Ipikai Poetry Journal in 2024. David then translated the poem to Shona language.

Maramba Doro

Pandinopedza kukwekweta hari yemadzisahwira
Shavi rangu riye remaramba doro ndiye tugu
Ndotanga chikudo changu chiye
Ndokuma homu homu
Kunge bveni radya chiwiro wiro
Ndotanga mhirizhonga pandari
Zvibhakera ndokanda kunge Kirimanjaro
Ndichipopota kunge rume rarambwa panhaka
Ndini Botso, murume wemusindo

Kana ndahudzatsa hwemadzisahwira
Kana nyadzi handisisina, pasi tsve
Ndotuka nevasina mhosva
Zuro ndakatuka Tezvara
Kuti mwana wake itsimbe
Inobika mbodza

Rimwezuro ndakaigochera pautsi;
Mai vakanditsiura kuti, 'Mwanangu, rega doro. Wava chiseko chenyika.'
Ini ndokupindura pfocho,
'Munotaurisa imi amai. Doro handirege kusvika muguva.'

Kana ndahudhudhudza hwemadzisahwira
Kana kadembo kanonhuwa ndino vhiya paruzhinji
Kuna hembe dzinetsvina ndinonanika paruvanze
Shavi remaramba doro rinonditambudza
Kana waya dzemumusoro mangu dzadamburwa nemhamba

Ndinenge ndokanyaira kunge ndakatenga nyika

Ndoimba chemutengure vhiri rengoro
Ndodzana kunge ngororombe yekwaMrewa

Maramba doro angu aya achandipinza
Muna taisireva, ndigo torerwa mudzimai navaTezvara
Kana kuripiswa kutuka Mai
Ndouwanepiko, nhai hamawe, mushonga wekurapa
Shavi rangu iri remaramba doro?

Binge Drinking Blues

Once I down Masese brew
I lose my marbles
Possessed by a bingeing spirit
And prance around like a baboon
High on wild fruits
I search for the weak to bully
When I am drunk on booze
And itch for a good fight,
Rubble Rouser is my nick name

Yesterday I got slaughtered
And pissed off my father-in-law
When I taunted his daughter
For being a waste of space
And a poor cook

The day before
I told my mother
To get on her bike
When she warned me about my bingeing
I didn't give a toss
About the mother's curse

Once I binge drink
I don't care about hanging
The family's dirty linen in public
I'm too tipsy to give a damn
I love to sing without shame

Where will my binge drinking blues lead me?

To the bottom of the deep sea?
Or down and out on the canvass?
Or my mother throws me out
And I sleep rough on the streets?
Where can I get the pill
That heals my binge drinking blues.

Kouma naani (quatre parole)

I.

Kabourou yé dibi yé
I té miri
O fana yé dibi finmamba
Dinin maw ta to an na
Masa yɛrɛ ta to an na
O fila dabiri le ne an na miri dala
I ba fɔ fara dabiri lén kɔlon kan

Yɛlɛko ye mana mana ko ba le ye
Nga mana mana mɔgɔ te se
Ki i bla a fɛ
A te se ka yɛlɛ a kan fana
Yɔrɔ koun kan ko fana bé tén

Dinin maw fana ka sabali sa tén
Masa yɛrɛ ba don
Masa de Masa ye

Né Fa !!!
Ni ne ye sigui ka miri ye
An ta fa ye an ta ba yé fana
Nɔtɛ na yan fa ye a be ko camman dɔn
Nɔtɛ na yan ba ye a be ko camman dɔn

II.

Aw né ka djonya kai, a bènna o bolo
Aw ma tiyen a laa nɔtɛ a bènna o bolo

Dounia kow ka tchan a bènna a bolo
Nga Kɔrɔdouga bi yala a bènna a bolo fana
Alisa djon ya niwa, aw té sabaliwa
Aw yé ya fa té sa, aw té sabalisa
Diyén yé limaniya so yé, aw té sabaliwa
Aw ya degui djigai mina, aw té sabalisa

Monnè té tèmai ni kan
Aw ya famou
Ni kan
Ni kan sa
Ni Kan aw ya famou
Oya fɔ aw yé
Aw yé o ya fɔ
Aw ya famou

O tan ta aw kisɛla
A ŋingɛ lénbɛ
Aw yɛrɛ tan yɛrɛ toyi
A ŋingɛ lénbɛ
Fîn ya té ko dougou yé
Nga o ya ŋingɛ dɛ

III.

Kɔnɔ bɛ kan ka kaci na lon ko yé
N'dén
N'dén diyen bé tan né
Ni mi ka donni sôrô
O bi dabiri tɔw dala
O te miri an tɔwla
An mɔgɔw !!

Fatɔ mousso te fili a dén man
N'té fîn fɛ ani fana n'tɛ gɛman Fɛ
Yali boula lé yirali la wa ?
Miri te fosi glan
Nga nan bé ta na bara yé
A bé fin canman yira an na

Aw bésé bi, aw be na sé lon dɔ
Fɔ ta yɛrɛ ban
Nga diarra té kaci na séko yé
A be kaci na dankan de ye

Fitri walé ya yé dɔlɔ yé
I kani i mi ka fa ala
Ni bɔla tɔrɔla.

IV.

Ni fɔgnon koun yé yéfin
An koun ba yé ka ŋa téré fɛ
Kow bé dougou la soufɛ
A té yé
Fɔgnon taa ka sira bila ni téré ka bɔ
A be tɛmin na ka sira o togo l'a soufɛ

Ni tara farafina
Djonni té djinninya kɛ
An té soŋali kɛ
An té galo tigai kɛ...
Olou bé calé djo kan
O ta bɔ ka doun

O té grin-grin
A bé sé ka karaba

Kon Ka wili té kon ka sé yé
O to yé
Nikan ko de be bɔ
O be bɔ
Ko be n'kɔnɔ te sounɔgɔ
A ba nikan ko le bɔ yɔrɔ ŋini nan
A tɛ
Nikan ko le tolo ka gɛlɛ
Wa a te siran
Nga a foura toubé
Ségou boliba naani bolo...
A koun bé ten (C'était comme ça)

Waati dɔ l'a
A koun bé si mɔgɔ l'a
Ka fɔ ko dinin ŋɛ mɔgɔ
Ki dabɔ politiki ko l'a ?

Fagan koun bi djoufran
Dinin ŋɛ mɔgɔw koun bi djoufran
Djamanandenw koun bi djoufran
I akili koun bi djoufran

Awɔ !!! Miri bi faasa
Kɔnkɔ bi faasa
Nɛw bi faasa
I yɛrɛ da d'y i faasa

I bé kɛ soubaga yé

I bé kɛ mangoni yé
I bé kɛ dala mɔgɔ yé
I bé kɛ manchidon bali yé

Awɔ ni bɛ !!!
I bé miri bali yé
I bé tachi bali yé
I bé gouman don bali yé

Nga bi o ban dali
Ani ka an nan akili yira
Nongon naa koun mina
O ka kan ka o da do ala

Awɔ o ban dali
Ka yira ko ben jamanan
Kɔnɔ o yo koun ko

Awɔ ni yé dinin mɔgɔ yé
Masa ka ci lase lila
A soumané né a kɔ

A soumané né a lamin bagaw kɔ
A soumané né jamanandenw kɔ
A soumané né an bɛ kɔ

E mandon diyen yɛlɛmanan
Ow ban dali
Dinin ŋɛ mɔgɔw ban dali

Ow ban dali
Ka sɔrɔ kounou

Ow yé Jordano Bruno djéni ni ta yé

Ka sɔrɔ kounou
Ow yé Spinoza fara kabɔ mɔgɔw la

Ni bɛ
Hakilina hɔrɔnyalen kama

Foyi téyi (il n'y a pas de problème)

A ma dabɔ kɛlɛ kama nga n'dimina
Ni kɛlɛ ma ban bana ba ban nga n'dimina
Mɔgɔ ta don icomi Allah nga n'dimina
I djougou ya foci te n'kɔnɔ nga n'dimina
Ni ya kɛ bɛ ladili yé
I ba don ko dambé te bɛ la

Ali ni yi mougnou icomi dougoukolo
Ki mougnou icomi yiri bé na falén ila
Mɔgɔ be sɔrɔ ka sini kan fo iyé
Ma ci kana sini kan fo n'ŋé

Ali niyé kilé ban sounɔgɔ la
Nkɔrɔ
Ma be sɔrɔ mi ŋɛ blénné né i kɔrɔ
Ali ni n'ta blénna n'ta fɔ iyé
Laban né djɔrɔ bé n'na
Nba don

Ni n'ma sɔrɔ i mako ta la
Allah téna djigui kana kouma
Mɔgɔci fɛ i kɛ walé la
I bo don ?
Ni n'ŋɛ blénna n'bé ségui so

Ni kɛlɛ béyi kaban
Kouma te yi mi te taa kan
Djiyén yé tolo yé
N'bé ségui so
Ali ni n'té tolo sɔrɔ yi

Sɛ bé Masa dé yé

Miri (Pense)

Kɔnɔ mi bi ban kassiman
Kan ka miri guinguin nan
Alé te kassi ka ko ja mɔgɔ yé
Alé be kassi na dambé de yé
Alé be kassi na dɔnko de yé
Alé be kassi na seko de yé
Masa yo de kalifa alé la
Ni yo famou o ŋanan

Soufɛ kassi te ma kɛ soubaga yé
A man ka kɔnɔ kɛ soubaga yé
A makan ka boukan kɛ soubaga yé
Nga ni guinguin ya yɛrɛ bla a dambé
Fɛ dron a ma fɔ alé soubaga
Ka ŋinin an djogow kɔ
Ko dogo kagnan

Nɔtɛ mɔgɔ be dén ladjé la soufɛ
A ba ba ladjé la
Mɔgɔ te dén ladjé la soufɛ
A ba ba ladjé la
Nga a te na mɔgɔci akili la ko dén souma yé

Ni yo famou
A ba dabila ka ka da
Babili ŋinikali kɛ guinguin nan

Na tounou na
O te sé ko ta o
Wa a ta bla yɔrɔ don

Mɔgɔ kan ka sé i yɛrɛ là
O de la bamananw ba fɔ : I yɛrɛ lon.
Awɔ ni yi yɛrɛ lon
I bé ko camman don

Sankoï
Jeli nounou kan ka ni famou
O kan ka ni fɔ
O kan ka koulé ni ni yé
Diyen sera yɔrɔmina ni
A kan ka tɔgɔ tiyen dabila

Djonni ya fɔ ? Né tɔgɔ bɔlaye
O man kan kɛ koun kɔrɔta i bɔlɔ
Ya ni a ka sé o man i kan ka sé
I dabara la ani i yɛrɛ la

Poyi kê (faire la poésie)

Kouma kaanŋi kouma tigui le da
Dou kaanni doutigui le bolo
Dougou kaanŋi dougoutigui le bolo
Nga poyi kaanŋi bɛ bolo

A yé salaya dabila
Poyi kɛla kan ka kouma
Poyi kɛla kan ka kaci comi kɔnɔ
Poyi kɛla kan ka yada ni koumaden yé

Poyi kɛ ni maloya te bɛn
Poyi kɛ ni makoun te bɛn
Poyi kɛ ni miribaliya te bɛn
Poyi kɛ ni kelenan kaci te bɛn

Awɔ

A be kaci kounmina
A kan ka ko o sɛbɛn
A be miri kounmina
À kan ka ko o sɛbɛn

Ô Kouma

Kana dimi do poyi l'a
Kana dimi do i l'a miri l'a
Kana poyi bla kelenan kaci yé
Kana poyi bla maloya yé

Ô...

Kani i makoun maloya yé
Kani i makoun a kɛ kelenan kaci yé
Koulé i ka sɛbɛ kɔnɔ

Kana siran kelenan miri ŋɛ
O yé poyi taagana de yé

Kana siran kelenan taama ŋɛ
O yé poyi taagana de yé

Kana siran kelen ya ŋɛ
Poyi yɛrɛ de tén
Lomi mɔgɔw benni kan mɛ
O bé nan famou

I yɛrɛ be nan famou
Ko poyi bé bara kɛ dougou kɔnɔ
Ko poyi bé bara kɛ kounkolo kɔnɔ
Ko poyi bé bara kɛ nin kan

Kani sanka poyi ma
Poyi kaangni na tigui yé
Poyi kaangni na kalan baga yé
Poyi kaangni ni poyi kɛbaga yé

Usman Danjuma Osu (Nigeria): Poems in Iloyi (Ejiri/Afo)

LOH PWAH KWOYAH MI

Gba-a koya mi ku fya ipwah mah
La ki wuh enyeh wa rima wo-o mbole mu eyi 'yi onu
Khangheruweh ng-ira kele la ozenga mah
Ongala 'wu eshi 'yi enzuh ibimah ole lu pyah lungho wa mu-u
la edumah wu iwomo, la ingiwu langi-langi wu m'onu ombahmbah
'wu oduhduh 'wu-Onijiriya nzu ole, ifyeh ligba li fye la ubu-uruwu la kudapeh
la akpa-la akpa, la igima la olu 'wu-esheshih; ira la ibi emba
No asangah yi kudapeh nzu iyi anyih foo me-e;
Irih igbo kwofih ngu lukwu nduh kishere yi.
Gba imene ila esuh egu mu ijalu aku kaneh la oduhduh, iyi kasa mo
njiii obo zo te aku kiya ngi iduma, imasa ma mo. Kwonyi kuyi
Eyi ifulomo mo; aku ivongo ma iyi owuru wu uyi ewo-ilomo mo
Ototo 'wu-akor oduwu ma mu igbaroh sho-o
mo uwuh kenzu la igima, enzuh mi ! Enzuh mi !! onyeh aku shoro-shoro

GRANT MY REQUEST

If my request be granted
Let's wipe these incessant tears on the face of the sun
Let the caressing irony be disenchanted
and these days' human heads harvest cease it's fan
from the dutiful veins and reins of the Nigerian nation's north.
Let us allow the return of the piece of our aesthetic peace
rooted in our love for values' volumes and worth
The knuckles of our peace are diseased to decease
Waiting to soon wipe us away on the whole,
Targeting brotherhood's eardrum for a kill has no essence
for attendant eulogy priding the self bold;
but a show and practice of abject nonsense
If from the bottom of our heart love and truth be praised
my people ! My people...!! Let banner of love be once raised

YIMOH-RIMAH ALUGBAGA

Kuyeh ngu mi ku ulugbaga awu egbomi mi shiyi enzu mbakor
mba bokor oma etu yi eshieshi mbala akpahna momor,
akweyi onongor mi ma
mari-mari mba bokor oma imgbomoh ma mi momor.
Immi mbala eguh mi ki bulohmah la jeri-jeri ito ika.
Mu-udu kiyi eyi epe-po, akeyi makor kuyi kunyi
Tayih gba-a kiri inzu mbeshi mbala ubwu-kodomgblo
Kwofi ngu onene lunyi luh yi eyi epo m'akor, ibo la inyashi
Ubwu-idomoh yi a wirima eshie yi ido-o-o;
Onu yi ola de mo akwei ubomo le pah
Nghoma no she ! La lu yi mo lu nghoma she kala iyi ikwu mo lin-ndama.

ARISE, YOUTH TODAY

When I was a youth I sold my heart to the elders
who saw the pores inmy heart's skin as receptive enough
to send their corrections when in me they saw any error
There with my peers we grew hugging virtue and values.
Our foreheads had two each but our heart had
One eye so we romanced with confident contentment
Today, your heart's eyes are double and as such, troubled
And contentment has left your cage vacant and empty,
leaving your sun going down in the morning
Sit up! Sit well for repackaging for valid virtues and values.

Baxton Chipeta (Malawi): Poems in ChiChewa

NKHANZA ZA CHILENGEDWE

Kuwotcha kwa dzuwa kufunikila mthunzi
Uwu si mthunzi wamba chabe ayi
Koma obwera ndika mphepo ka yaziyazi
Koma ukamwaza maso, chilengedwe chidatha kuti psiti
Nalo dzuwa lichita kuwala mwa nkhwidzi
Mwina tili ku gahena, sitikudziwa chabe
Kamfuno, kuwawa kwa mutu ndi kuyima kwa ziwalo
Zikhala abwenzi athu apa mtima

Mitambo yakuda ichita msonkhano
Usiku onse mvula kugwa osalekeza
Naye kavuluvulu alowa m'bwalo
Nabala mphepo za mkuntho
Kutenga mizimu yosalakwa
Kumwamba kwatenga gulu nyengo iyi
Nyumba ndi milatho nazonso zitsanzika
Kusiya nkhawa komanso mavuto adzawoneni

Mmera ndi ziweto nazonso zisesedwa
Podalira pokhapo pomwe alimi amalimbilapo mtima
Madzi odikha nawo adzetsanso mazangazime osaneneka
Mudzi onse pano wakhudzidwa ndi matenda;
Malungo, kutsekula m'mimba komanso kamwazi
Apa tsono ndipamayambiliro chabe
Nkhondo zenizeni zibwera posachedwapa
Njala ndi imfa!

CRUELTY OF NATURE

The scorching heat of the sun calls for a shade,
Not just an ordinary shadowy sanctuary,
But with a comforting breeze
Looking around, no single vegetation is in existence
The rays of the sun are fierce
Or maybe it's hell, we just don't know it yet
Nosebleeds, headaches, and strokes
Keep us company at all times.

Heavy and dark clouds gather
It rains throughout the whole night
A whirlwind joins the dance
Giving birth to cyclones
Taking with them innocent souls
Heaven gains many this time around
Buildings and bridges unravel
Leaving nothing but stress and burdens.

Crops and livestock are swept away
The only hopes farmers were left with
Stagnant waters bear plagues
The whole community is entangled in;
Malaria, cholera and Typhoid fever
This is just the beginning though
The real tragedies will really strike soon,
Hunger and death!

NDINALI POMPO

Ndinali pompo,
Eya, ndinatsuka maso angawa
Pomwe kadzuwa kachidzulodzulo kadatitsanzika
Kumilira kuseri kwa mapiri a Bvulumende
Ndipo posakhalitsa, m'dima udatilandira
Kuwopseza makosana kuti tiwone msana wa njira
Ndipo ine ndidayima chilili ngati sungwi
Kuwonkhetsa khobidi la tsiku limenelo

Ndinali pompo!
Pomwe chidakwacho chinatulukira
Dzandidzandi ngati mwana ophunzira kuyenda
Chitafinya kabanga wake pa mtima pake
Mahutala adalira ngati tambala okhwima kumene
Makosana adakuwa natukwana zakukhosi kwawo
Ana adapeza chowonela ndipo adapulumutsa mtereche
Amayi adangoti kukamwa pululu ndipo kukadalowa ntchetche
"Kodi ndi mamuna wa yani uyu?"
Mapilikanilo angawa adamva akunong'onezana

Ndinali pompo,
pomwe gareta laliwiro lidandidutsa
Woyendetsa adayesetsa kudongolera
Mathero ake adalipila nazo moyo wake ndi ena atatu;
Amayi, kamwanapiye kawo komanso njonda ina
Maso angawa adawona ngozi yonse
Pomwe galimotolo lidakayima
Ndipo posakhalitsa tidamva
Eya, phokoso logonthetsa mmakutu la ambulasi.

I WAS THERE

I was there,
Yes, I was present
When the orange hues of the sun kissed goodbye
Descending below Bvulumende hills
In a twinkle of an eye, dusk smiled at us
Threatening every folk to wind up;
Their unfinished endeavors
So was I,
Summing up the coins for the day.

I was there!
When the drunkard condensed abruptly
Strolling back and forth on the busy lane
His booze held firmly to his chest
Cars horned from all directions
Folks booed and cursed in all languages
Kids watched as the drama unfolded
Ladies were left mouth agape;
"Whose husband is this?"
I almost heard them whisper.

I was there,
When the over-speeding vehicle,
Swept past me
The driver tried to miss the over drunken fellow
In the process, costing his life and of three others:
A mother, her toddler and another man
My naked eyes witnessed the whole tragedy
As the minibus halted to a crash
And in a blink of an eye we heard it,

Yes, the deafening sound of the blaring ambulance.

CHIFUKWA CHIYANI?

Kuyesetsa umu ndi umu
Kukakamiza nako kosayamba
Kuti mwina zinthu ndikuyendako
Kulemba m'madzi akuwerenga ndi achule
Kukakamiza nkhutukumve
Mwana wosayamika
Wotenga chuma cha makolo ake ngati chake
Opusitsidwa ndi khalidwe laku Ulaya
Kusintha kwa iye ndi mbiri ya makedzana

Waphunzira sukulu zodula kwambiri
Makwacha kulowetsa pazokhumba zilizonse
Kuti ulemelero ugwe kumwamba kufika pansi pano
Koma umuwona uyo akutulukira pa zenela
"Kupatulako moyo, zina zonse zimakhala kwa muyaya"
Awo ndiwo maganizo ake
Ndiye achitilanji
Kugwira ntchito ngati ndi kapolo?
Pomwe magalimoto opuma
Akhala ngati maluwa m'munda pakhomo lakwawo

Koma imbwana ameneyi amadziwa?
Kuti winawake akusala tulo
Kusakasaka ya mchere ndi fizi
Chifukwa nthawi iliyonse akhoza kuwona msana wa njira.

BUT WHY

Through fire and rain
The persuasion's unwavering
To reach the finishing line
But at what cost?
For someone who's numb,
Unappreciative.
Considering his parent's wealth as his own
Brainwashed by the western culture
Not ready to be civilized
For what?

Been through expensive private schools
Dime spent on every luxury
To make his life a paradise on earth
Still, he runs away from school
'Everything except life lasts forever'
That's his logic
So why would he,
Work himself to death?
With all the whips,
Filling up the parking lot

But does he know?
That someone's struggling
To secure a place
cause the tuition issue,
Has been on the neck.

ABWANA

Tawona kathupi kako kosalala
Dzina lililonse ndayenela kukutchula
Sindikusamala zoti siwe mkazi wakunyumba
Komano nthawi inayake ukhoza kukhala
Inetu sindikukunyoza
Pano katakwe ndine osati iwe
Ntchitoyi ukuyifuna kapena ayi?

Tasuzumila timalova tonseti
Ufuna uzakhalenso ngati iwo?
Iweyotu chisankho ulibe
Koma kundibwereka mapilikanilo akowo
Ntchafu zako zopereka mudyo ndikazithila chipenyero
Kamwa langa likungochita dovu
Ndikangosuzumila mapapaya akowo pamtimapo
Ntchitoyi ukuyifuna kapena ayi?

Tsonotu iwe utseke pakamwa
Izi ndi za awiri basi
Chani? Ukanena kutiko?
Palibe akakumvele kanyembete iwe
Zitheka? Tiyeni tichite machawi basi
Ndimadziwa ine kuti ntchitoyi umayifuna iwe.

THE GREEDY MANAGER

Look at your body cutie pie
I deserve to call you any names honey
Who cares that you're not my wife?
Sooner or later you might be
Don't consider me scorning you
For I am in charge here not you
Do you want the job or not?

Look at all those unemployed graduates
Do you want to end up just like them?
You leave yourself with no choice
But to dance to every tune of mine
Your thighs are appetizing to stare at
My mouth can't stop watering
By just gazing at your breasts
Do you want the job or not?

Don't let this go out of that door
It's between the two of us
What? You will report where?
Nobody will buy your lies
Yes? Let's make it quick then
I knew you badly wanted the job.

Iwuagwu Ikechukwu (Nigeria): Poems in Igbo

ANYỊ NILE BỤ OBERE CHI

Mgbe uche gị riri oto nwa agbohobia nke dina n'elu hekta nke akwụkwọ amamihe, ma anya gị rie naanị mma ya n'ụlọ nzukọ echiche
Ị chere na i meriela ya?
Chere ruo mgbe ị huru ka eluigwe n'atabiri gi anya n'egbu amuma, na egbe eluigwe n'agbasìkè igosi n'eluigwe n'akwụsị ịkwa ákwá, ma ọ bụ igu osisi nkwụ na-agbakọta ọnụ n'usoro nụkwụ ifufe nke n'aku ekwe okochi.
Ma eleghị anya, mgbe ị hụ ụtụtụ na-apụta na-abịa n'olu nnụnụ na-eti mkpu, okuko n'eti mkpu na ahiha igirigi di na ya, ma o bu mgbe mgbede na-adakwasị anyi site n'ụda si n'ọnụ ụmụ-ukpala, nkwa mgbe ọnwa na-egwu egwu n'azụ osisi ekwe-achara na ogwe iroko.
Ma eleghị anya, I ga echere ruo mgbe ị hụuru ụmụ agbọghọ mara mma n'akpụkpọ ụkwụ ha na mkpịsị ụkwụ ha, na-egosi na ha mụtara okwu n'ọnụ igba ntuli egwu, ma ọ bụ mgbe ị ga aga *Idanre*, ebe Ogun bi, onye di ma n'agaghari n'elu n'ugwu, na ọdọ mmiri nne Idoto, ebe mgbịrịgba na osisi Okigbo di; uru ụra nke ọdịdị.
Nti gị o nụla uda olu enyi na-akpọ, mbigbo odụm, na enwe na-akpa mkata? Ma ọ bụ anya gị ohụla anụ ọhịa dị ka mgbada na-agba ọsọ n'azụ ụkwụ ya dị larịị, na-apụ n'ụzọ gbagọrọ agbagọ ka ha na-agba ọsọ pụọ n'anya anụ ọhịa nwere ike iri ha?
Emume gị bụ akwa e ji mara ekele na mma, akpụkpọ ahú gị dị mma; na-adọrọ anya n'anya nde mmadụ.

Nne anyị Africa! Nnukwu oke nne-nwanyị!
Leopold dere n'akwụkwọ, ihe ọ hụrụ n'anya n'ọji gị mara-nma,
ojii anyị, omaricha ojii dị ka unyi ọkụ.
Igbo, Hausa, Yoruba, Asante, Ewe, Fante, Twi, Massai, Himba, Zulu, Khoisan, Ndebele, Samburu na nke unu niile

Anyị nile bụ obere chi.

WE TOO ARE GODS

When your mind has captured her nudity laying supine on acres of encyclopedias, and your eyes only eaten her beauty in the parliament of imagination
You feel you've conquered her?
Wait till you see the fluffy clouds winking with silent lightning, and the growling of thunder marking the disappearance of weeping skies, or Palm fronds colliding in conspiracy, lured on by the billowing breezy beats of harmattan
Maybe when you witness the breaking of dawn heralded by tweeting of birds, crowing of cockerels and swaying of dew-laden grasses, or the descent of dusk marked by a deluge of chirping melodies from the larynx of crickets, and the moon's hide and seek game behind bamboo stems and giant iroko arms
Perhaps you might wait till you see maidens whose feet and ankles clad in beaded glory reaffirm their mastery of the alphabets in the throat of the drums or till you visit *idanre*[1] , the abode of Ogun, dweller of the hills and mother idoto's grotto, the abode of *Okigbo's*[2] iron bell and stick; nature's pillow.
Have your ears been littered with the trumpeting of elephants, roaring of lions, and chattering of monkeys in the safari? Or your eyes sighted antelopes priding themselves on swift slender hinds, darting away from preying predators?

---

[1] A beautiful landscape located in Ogun State, Nigeria

[2] Renowned Igbo poet killed during the Biafran war

Your ritual is a tapestry of awesomeness and intricate beauty,
your rind, clad in splendour; alluring to a billion eyes
Oh, Mama Africa! Cradle of mankind!
Leopold spilled on paper, his witness of your black beauty,
our blackness, beautiful black coals.
*Igbo, hausa, Yoruba, Asante, Ewe, Fante, Twi, Massai,
Himba, Zulu, Khoisan, Ndebele, Samburu*[3] and yours

We too are gods

---

[3] Some tribes in Africa

NNE BU IHE
(maka RitaNgozi Iwuagwu)

Nwanyi aka igwe ike n'adighi agwu-agwu, kedu ka m g'esi kele gi?
Gi, obere chi buru'm nafo onwa itoolu
Onye ndu nke mbu'm. I ji aka gi luo agha uwa wotere gi, ma nwekwa ume iji kuo'm
E chetere'm:
I n'ezuru m n'aka nnukwu ura, kpoputa'm n'ezi ebe eluigwe n'atupiara anyi anya dika chi oro ezo site na ijeri kpakpando.
N'ebe ahu, nime emume ozuzo na ochucho nke onwa, I ga ebido guwa abu "Twinkle Twinkle little star..." n'olu bekee, ebe olu'm di ntakiri n'eso n'uzo mmuta. N'agbanyeghi n'amaghi m ihe di iche n'etiti ukwe n'iru uju, okwu gi wee buru abu n'ime okpukpu nti m na isi ihe di n'ime m.
Ugbua, k'afo iri-ato gacharala, ahuru m anya gi ka o na-aduba m obi dika agiga si adupu balloon, nchegbu gi bu chi gbachiri nkiti nke na esoghari m. Mana I na-atughari ekpere n'ime uwe m, tuba ha n'akpa m di ka ego elegharala anya. Mkpuruokwu ndi na-esi n'egbugbere onu gi na-aga n'elu ihunanya – 'I riela nri?' Olu gi – balm nke na-ebelata ihe mgbu'm.
Ite gi bu ulo igba egwu ebe ofe gi na-agba egwu dika Michael Jackson. Obuna obere ch di iche iche ga ahapu onodu ha ka ha we rie ofe I siri, ma o bu ngaji nke amamihe jollof gi
Oh Nnem!
Enwere amaokwu mkpisi ode m n'agahi enwe ike ikwuputa, nihi, nihi na ha na-eleda udi gi anya mgbe niile. Ma ahiri ndi a di umeala n'obi, nke edere n'elu akwukwo a buru ibu , bu libations, o bughi maka iru uju, kama ofufe nke RITA – obere chi nwanyi ka na-aga ije.

Ka kpakpando buru onye akaebe: Nwanyi ahu kuru abu n'ime abali, na usekwu ya na-aga n'etiti anyi, na-ekuba oku n'okpukpu umu mmadu.

MOTHER IS THE LIGHT
(for Rita Ngozi Iwuagwu)

Woman of iron wrists and dawn-swept resolve, how do I carve your person into breath?
You, the deity that housed my liquid essence for nine moons.
First priestess of my becoming. You cradled the world in those spent palms, and still had
the stamina to cradle me.
I remember:
You would abduct me from the arms of slumber, and pilot me into the oracle of night, where the
fluffy dark sky winks its billion eyes of stars at us like secret gods. There, in the ritual hide and
seek game of the moon, your voice would reel out a chant "Twinkle, twinkle little star..."
while my tiny voice recaps in learning steps. Though I could barely discern rhyme from dirge,
your words carved poetry into the bones of my ears and essence of my being.
Now, at twenty-nine seasons trod, I feel your eyes piercing my doubts like needle to a
balloon, your worry is the silent god that stalks me. Yet you fold prayers into my clothes,
tuck them in pockets, like overlooked currencies. The syllables marching from your lips upon the
boulevard of love—"Have you eaten?" Your voice - the balm that soothes my pain away.
Your pot is a theatre where stews dance like *Michael Jackson,* condiments and flames conspire
and bow to your culinary whims. Even gods would decast and kneel for a taste of your *afang*

soup, for a spoonful of your jollof wisdom.
Ah, *Nne'm*.
There are verses my ink can't confess, for they will always underemphasize your sole thumps.
But these humble lines, etched upon this vast blank, are libations, not for grief, but for worship
of RITA - a goddess still walking.
Let the stars bear witness: the woman who sowed poems into night, and cooked galaxies in her
kitchen still walks among us, breathing fire into the bones of men.

Ismail Bala (Nigeria): Poems in Hausa

Yawon Duniya

Jiya a yawon duniya
Na hadu da karamin mutum
Zan rera waka ga mai so na
Mai ajiyar karamin mutum
Dan lele zo mu yi lilo mu gangaro
Alawa ga zaki ga gardi
Sai karamin mutum

Yaushe za ka ziyarci fadata
Don nayi maka shimfidar lagwada
Ya mai so na
Sadaukar min da karamin mutum
Don na ga fararen taurari.

The Voyage

In my voyage in yesteryears
I met the small statured one
One who loved me and for whom I sing a song
The keeper of the small one
The affectionate one come go with me
Oh you the sweet and the delicious
Oh you the small one

When shall you come see my palace?
When do you come for a grand treat?
Oh you my lover
Give me yourself the small one
Come give me ecstasy

Haruffai Shida

Haruffai shida masu fararen furanni
Na yi kitso da tsagun ko wane daya

Harafi na daya: inibin raina
Sukari a shafin kirjina

Mangwaro koshi babu
Abarba gidan zaki

Idon basirana
Lafazin rayuwata

Malam bude littafi
tarbo min haruffan nan shida

Kafin na rikice

The Six Letters

Six letters with white flowers
Each being a part of me

One is the vineyard of my soul
The second the sugar of my heart

The third an insatiable fruit
The fourth is oozing juice

The fifth is my intellect
The sixth the basis of my existence

Open your book and
Lead me to the six letters

Lest I vanish.

Barin Zuma

Sannu sannu zan bi gabobinka dai bayan dai
Amma sai nai maka barin zuma
Sannan harshe na ya bika da lasa
Tun daga sama har kasa
Ba inda zan bari face sai na cimma burina
Sai ka narke gumin jikinka
Ya kashe min kishi.

A Sweet Lick

Slowly I'll go down your limbs
After I've covered you in honey
My tongue shall roll over you
Up and down
Leaving out no portion of you
Till I devour your sweat
And quench my thirst.

Yanci

Nonuwana sun cika sun yi nauyi
Suna begen hannayenka
Kai kadai ka iya rikesu
Tamkar kana rike da kwai
Kai ka iya murza su kamar amaro
Ka iya shan su kamar lemu
Yaya zanyi da raina?
Ai ba sauran budurci a tare da nonuwa na
Tun ranar da ka ba su 'yanci
Basu san kowa ba sai kai.

Freedom

Full and heavy my breasts
Yearn for your touch
You know best how to handle them
In a delicate way
In a firm squeeze
And juicy suckle
Oh my my
No more uninitiated they are
For you've set them free
Knowing no one but you.

Gwagwarmayar Kauna

Na bude idona
Haske kamar na walkiya ya keto
Don ganinka.

Lebe na karkarwar murna
Baki zai sha zumar bakin masoyi
Kai!

Irin wannan lagwada
Ga zuma
Ga kuma madara za ta kwarara

Jiki fa ya rude
Samun natsuwa fa sai masoyi da masoyiya
Sun dulmiya a cikin gwagwarmayar kauna

Sai sun hade. . .

The Love Battle

My eyes wide open
Full of glimmer
Just to behold you

The tremor in my lips
Grows, anticipating a kiss
From a lover, oh!

What a delicacy
How sweet
Such flowing cream

The trembling soul
Knows no peace till lovers meet
And delve in the battle of love

Together. . .

Masaka Madeda (Kenya): Poems in Kidawida

Icho Chai Chiao?

Icho chai chaiswa chayaa?
Chiredo chinyughilo anyaa,
Chai chiche chirumbuto shwaa,
Chiredenyi chipunguze mbeo.
Icho chai sena chaduaa?
Chisewikirilo ndedlalaa,
Chisechue kii ndedghalaa,
Chidungo chidpunguzire mbeo.
Icho chai mwachienja haa?
Mwachinywa chose musetalaa,
Chikaka chasia ni balaa,
Chideka chidifunyire mbeo.
Icho chai chiao abaa?
Nechi nicho chofi ughu mtaa,
Chedu dadachinywa kila saa,
Nicho difunyaa nacho mbeo.
Chai cheko msedidungiaa?
Chikaruda ndeditoshekaa,
Se chikasinga ndedikatwaa,
Desindachinywa difunye mbeo.

Where is this Tea?

Where's the tea been passed to?
Let it be drank right here,
Let it be slurped fast!
Bring it, let it put away the cold.
Do we still have tea?
If we don't we won't sleep,
If the cups aren't full we won't home,
Pour it, let it put away the cold.
Where have you taken the tea to?
You drank it all? We know you might -
If there's no tea, there's trouble;
Let tea be, it puts away the cold.
Where's the tea, man?
You know it's the kibangara1 in these parts,
Here, we drink it every time,
It's what puts away the cold.
Come on, isn't tea not there?
If it's appetizing, we'll keep drinking,
If it's sweet, we'll keep drinking,
All day long, to put away the cold.

Mwai wa Kidawida

Nekwanee na mwai wa kidawida,
Waghokaa jinsi wakushinga poda,
Ngawona siendaa nkimila mada.
Nikamuroghua kwasinda pinana?
Inimoni Masaka neko pinana,
Simanyire oho niwada nge bwana.
Nemzera kedu ni viangachinyi,
Kolughu mzedu dadalima vichinyi,
Na isi machi dadadaya modenyi.
Nemkota mzenyu ni hao wele,
Ni koisi Kishushe kwa chovu tele,
Amu kombayi Woi kwa makelele?
Nkamkota ni Mwatate makongenyi,
Amu ni aisaa Bura iparenyi,
Amu kwenda cha Tuweta marughunyi?
Angu wele ni Mbololo iruwenyi,
Kama suwo ni Mghange Nyika mbeonyi,
Amu ngera Rong'e Juu mighondinyi…
Ela nashinikie ngashinika,
Nezerwa wei, "sikuelewei kaka,
Jamani Kitaita sijakishika".
Ikachabidi niende chia rapo,
Nechadima nachiwada charo chapo,
Ngakazana sejhi nakumbilwa pepo.

The Beautiful One from Taita

I once met a Taita girl,
A beauty in a powdered face,
Thought me, today I won't just ogle.
I greeted her, hi! How's your day?
I'm Masaka and I'm fine,
How about you my dear?
Said me, I come from the place of pines,
Where vegetable patches abound,
We fetch water straight from the river.
I asked her where she came from;
From down in Kishushe, the place of elephants?
Or from the far away, noisy town of Voi?
From the sisal plantation of Mwatate?
Or the farmlands of Bura?
Or Taveta, the land of bananas?
Or is it Mbololo, the place of the hottest sun?
If not, Mghange Nyika, that cold place?
Or, maybe, from the hills of Rong'e Juu ...?
Then, I was surprised, so surprised;
When she said, "I don't understand you brother,
You see, I don't understand Kidawida."
So I had to go my way,
I decided to go my way,
I went away, like one possessed.

Marina gha Kidawida

Marina gha Kidawida, gheko ghisingie sana,
Mwakuleghwa, Mwakuida; Mwandangachu, Mwaluvuna,
Mara wei Kilumada, angu wei Mwakuwona.
Kuzoya weke Mwandisha, mpaka kwa Mwakisachi,
Mwakio, Dali, Mwakisha; Saru na Mwakiangachi,
Mara wei Mndwakisha, angu wei Mwawusuchi.
Kosikira wei Mbori, Mwapagha na Mkachia,
Mwaropo, Nyasi, Mwamburi; ela kawangwa wabia,
Mara wei Mwasufuri, angu wei Mwakusia.
Umu wawangwaa Zighe, ichai umu Mwambuwa,
Kilambo, Kai, Maseghe; Mwang'ombe na Me Kitawa,
Mara wei Mwakiseghe, angu wei Mwakuliwa.
Marina sa Mwakinyonyi, Mkakio na Mwavinyi,
Katarina, Mwamodenyi; Kiwanda, Mwamzinyi,
Mara wei Mwangandenyi, angu wei Mwambandenyi.
Na ghose ni gha mzinyi, ndewilaladamba nagho,
Masaka, Mwaisakenyi; Mwandoe, Mlagholagho,
Mara ni Msolowenyi, angu ni Mka - Masagho.
Gheko mengi sana ghamu, ghighorenyi ni ghiao,
Msekechadilaumu, weke abo weke mao,
Wei deghiwada ghamu, wei deliwa gha ao.

Kidawida Names

This poem celebrates the beauty of the sounds and different meanings of Kidawida names. The Wadawida community name their children after their grandparents (where a first born boy is named after the paternal grandfather, the first born girl is named after the paternal grandmother, the second borns are named after the maternal grandparents in this fashion, and so on), after the seasons in which they were born, after the peculiar traits they display at birth, naming is sometimes also influenced by emerging nearby cultures - where religion, intermarriages and modernisation may play a part - all in all, the names serve as a glimpse into the ways of life of the Wadawida people.

Male names mostly begin with the prefix Mwa-, while female names begin with Wa -, these mean 'the one who ...' Some female names also bear the prefix 'Mka-' which means 'wife of', usually a humorous way of 'marrying' the girl to the trait that describes her, especially a trade or a label that runs in the family.

Another similar prefix for female names is 'Mfu wa-' usually shortened to 'Mfwa-', it means 'daughter of' an assumption that the girl is born of or in the trait that so describes her. The latter is also used in informal names for the girls to name them with reference to their patronymic, in this case Mfwa Mwadime will be the daughter of the man called Mwadime. The male equivalent for son of so and so is 'Mndwa-', its literal translation is 'man of-'. Some Kidawida variations replace the Mwa- prefix with Ma-.

Mothers and fathers are called by the names of their first born children, whether or not these children are theirs biologically; for the mother, the prefix Me- precedes the name of the

firstborn to mean mother of, whereas Nde- precedes the name of the firstborn to mean father of.
The names mentioned in the poem include:
Mwakuleghwa: the unwanted, rejected one
Mwakuida: the passer by
Mwandangachu: the one with thin legs like the grasshoppers
Mwaluvuna: s/he of the live fence
Kilumada: the clingy one, clings like a bur
Mwakuwona: the seeing one
Mwandisha: the herdsman
Mwakisachi: the bushman, born in the bushes or around bushes
Mwakio: the one born at night
Dali: the pretentious one (prefixes are left out in some names)
Mwakisha: the careless one
Saru: fertiliser, with a prefix like Mwa- it would mean the fruitful one
Mwakiangachi: the palms guy
Mndwakisha: the son of the careless one
Mwawusuchi: the one who likes bone marrow
Mbori: the tearful one
Mwapagha: the one who takes blood (when people slaughter animals)
Mkachia: (wife of) the one on the road
Mwaropo: the hospitable one
Nyasi: grass, the one cuts or who does things with grass
Mwamburi: the one who keeps goats
Mwasufuri: the one with nothing
Mwakusia: the one with a diminishing effect.
Zighe: (usually with prefix) locust, born during a locust invasion
Mwambuwa: the one who tends to a farm

Kilambo: (usually with prefix) thing, the one with a
Kai: (usually with prefix) scum, the one with
Maseghe: the one with strong legs
Mwang'ombe: the one who keeps cows
Me Kitawa: mother of the girl without
Mwakiseghe: the hunter of skunks
Mwakuliwa: the forgetful ones
Mwakinyonyi: the birds lover
Mkakio: the wife of the night - comes home at dusk
Mwavinyi: he of the funny gums
Katarina: Catherine
Mwamodenyi: the one who loves the river
Kiwanda: (with prefix)kiosk, maker of
Mwamzinyi: the one who stays in his mothers house
Mwangandenyi: the guy by the wall, idler
Mwambandenyi: scorpion
Masaka: the bushman, born in a house of straw. Literally weeds
Mwaisakenyi: the bushman, the one who keeps to the bushes
Mwandoe: son of the soil
Mlagholagho: playfulness, the playful one
Msolowenyi: under the bed
Mka Masagho: wife of maize stalks, a woman who plants maize, wife of Masagho.

Wei ni Wacheambai

Weko wamu wichaa wikekalia wandu,
Wecha wikadakalia ni wacheambai,
Na wei wikekededeshwa ndewidikaa.
Weka wisemanyaa dewimanyire putu,
Dawichi ata wikubonye wanokombai,
Wizerenyi ni wukelu a ndewikataa.
Wana ata wisetalaa wei ni mwandu,
Wikakadeda welegha kimzedu mbai,
Ata wisefwaa waya wana wabang'aa!
Nichashoa changu nidame mwana wa mndu,
Na wisediredie wudawana na wai,
Muwizere wa huwo ndediwikundaa.
Nawemkotia sena wakundwa wakedu,
Wana wedu wikakawuya wacheambai,
Huwu kimzedu chiwaendangia haa?

That they're not from Around Here

There are some who lie to others,
That they are not from around here,
That when spoken to they won't respond.
But they know not that we know all about them,
Though they pretend that they are not from around here,
Tell them that they won't be enough[2]
Youth who don't even care it's a meeting,
They refuse to use our tongue,
They're not even ashamed, big children!
One day I'll take a stick and cane someone's child!
We don't want their youthfulness and girls here!
Tell them we don't want!
I ask you again my compatriots,
When all our children are not from around here,
Where will our tongue go to?

2 The not-enoughness here is an allusion to a vegetable or meat serving not being of the enough portion to be taken with msara/mswara, a staple food that is popular with the Wadawida (ugali/sima in Kiswahili) and many other communities in Kenya and other parts of Afrika, the side dish is usually of a smaller size.

Chumbo ra Kidawida

Basi loli raborelo, chumbo redu ra mzinyi,
Kuvine na kupoilo, kuramerame mezenyi,
Angu sena kuzamilo, kuvinie mabambenyi.
Kela se kwalusikire, ulujha lwa Kambe - Ndee?
Yani ulo kuseghore, losinga apana tee,
Lukakaborwa ni sere, kama ngolo isenee.
Sasa oko Kajogolo, wobora na ukabora,
Aboo kusekalilo, waborie nakuzera,
Ni chumbo sio mikalo, kusechokaa kuskira.
Na Aboo Sami Mwambi, naomoni waborie,
Uo mndu ni mghambi, gheko mengi ughambie,
Gha sukari na gha chumbi, kwa chumbo uriborie.
Oko Kifoto Habeli, ndedimliwaa jhingi,
Bendi yawo yedojali, lumi lodu 'chumba lungi,
Chumbo rikasinga kweli, wariichi wandu wengi.
Umu dawemkumbuka, ujha Aboo Mwamburi,
Olegheloghe ni mka, woweserieghe wori,
Uko Japan wendaftuka, ukaambalila mbori.
Basi loli raborelo, chumbo redu ra mzinyi,
Kuvine na kupoilo, kuramerame mezenyi,
Angu sena kuzamilo, kuvinie mabambenyi.

Kidawida Songs

Ah, they have been sang, songs of our homeland;
You'll dance and be merry, and jump up and down on the table,
Or if you want, you can dance on the rooftops.
Have you heard the one about Kambe's father?
Don't talk about it, it's the height of ecstasy,
Your heart will be at peace, if it wasn't.
There's Kajogolo, he sang and sang,
Let no one lie to you, he sang I tell you,
Songs not lies, you'll never tire to listen.
Then there's Aboo Sammy Mwambi, he too has sang,
That man is a sayer, and there's much he has said,
Some sugary and some salty, all in his songs.
And Aboo Habel Kifoto, we'll never forget him,
Their band really loved our tongue,
Their songs so sweet, many know them.
We'll also remember Aboo Mwamburi,
His wife left him, after all that waiting,
When she came from Japan, he almost cried.
Ah! They've really been sang, songs of our homeland,
You'll dance and be merry, and jump up and down on the table,
Or if you want, you can dance on the rooftops.

Obuchere James (Kenya): Poems in Luhya

OMWANA OMUSHE NIYAMEELA.

Omwana omushe niyameela
Litaala likwa liikuunda
Aha tsing'ombe tsianaanga
Bulaano haolelaanga!

Omwana omushe niyakoyana
Litaala lisikha pe
Abakoko nibatuukha beetsa
Kho benjira heena?

Ebindu biosi wasasia
Omukunda kwa papa wakusia
Ebiayo biosi biatsia
Hango hatong'a butswa!

Omwana omushe niyakoyaana
Kho litaala liosi liamayaana
Aobusangaali bwalingi
Bulano eshibeera neshingi.

Omwana omushe niyameela
Hango hatong'a kuru
Obulimo nende echindi mimera
Buayumba khumukuru.

WHEN THE LAST BORN IS A DRUNKARD.

When the last born son is a drunkard
The homestead remains desolate
Where cows once mowed
Now silence reigns.

When the last born son is a fool
Then the homestead is lost
When daughters come visiting
Where would they be hosted?

He has spoiled everything
He has sold the ancestral land
Even livestock is gone
Thus the home remains void.

When the last born son is abnormal
Then the homestead is lost
Where there was once laughter
Sorrow and gloom linger.

When the last born son is a drunkard
The homestead remains desolate
With grass and other weeds
Surrounding the old house.

Note: According to Luhya tradition, it's the last born son who remains in his parents' compound. Other sons have to move to other farms.

MWIKULU

Buli mundu yenyanga mwikulu
Aha obulafu bwakhanga
Aha abamalaika bembanga
Amayosi amalayi.

Buli mundu yenyanga mwikulu
Aha eshilima shibula
Aha amasika kabula
Kata eshibeela; kata inzala.

Mwikulu, aha abatakatifu benjila
Mwikulu, aha okhufwa khubula
Kata eminyakhano; kata olumbe.

Buli mundu yenyanga mwikulu
Aha khuli nende obunulu
Aha khubula olwikhuulu
Habula obusangaali bwonyene.

Buli mundu yenyanga mwikulu
Habula injila yokhutsia ebweneyo
Yaba inyeleele
Khandi indinyu.

HEAVEN

Everyone wants heaven
Where there's light
Where angels sing
Sweet, melodious songs.

Everyone wants heaven
Where there's no darkness
Where there are no tears
Nor sorrow; nor hunger.

Heaven, the home of saints
Heaven, where there's no death
Nor suffering; nor ailment.

Everyone wants heaven
Where there's pure bliss
Where there's no mourning
But only happiness.

Everyone wants heaven
But the way that leads there
Is but hard
And so narrow.

OMUHEELWA WANJE

Omuheelwa wanje
Yitsa hano
Yitsa undiile omukhono
Ekhuyile omanye abebusi banje
Khuboole aka liimenya.

Ekhuyile omanye ewuwo
Omanyane nende bamulamwa bo
Mana onalane ninabo
Nimweka amakhuwa amalayi.

Yitsa khusangaalile ebimuli
Nende amatsi amalayi
Nende amanyonyi
Nikeemba olwimbo olulayi.

Yitsa khutsie khu shikulu
Eshilikhwo obunulu
Ebiamu nende amatsi
Akanyira tsii.

Aha obushindu buhutsa
Nefu nikhumwenya butswa
Nikhutsunzuunana eminwa
Nikhuhulilisia obukhana...

Obwa tsiindochio
Nende omuchera
Nikuselenjela mwibanda
Nende khulwanda.

Yitsa undiile omukhono
Oli omuheelwa wanje
Oli eshimuli shianje
Oundi abulaho.

MY BELOVED

Come, my beloved
Come and hold my hand
Let me take you to my folks
For marital talks.

Let me take you to your new home
To introduce you to your inlaws
To get used to them
And learn much from each other.

Come, let's rejoice
As we admire flowers
And crystalline waters
And the melodious bird's song.

Let's go and tour the hill
That's full of thrill
As we munch on wild fruits
And quench our thirst with cool waters...

Where, amid a cool breeze
We'll hold hands and smile
Even as we exchange smooches
As we listen to the music...

Of the nightingale
And the winding river
Rolling down in the valley
And on boulders.

Come, hold my hand
You're my beloved
You're my flower
There's no other..

Rogers Lobeleng Sethole (South Africa): Poems in Sepedi

MPHE NAKO!

Pheladi mmušanoši pelong ya ka, mphe nako hle!
Mphe nako, pelong nnete eta go sa lla sa'go kaka maloba.
Pelong o sa dutše o nnoši, o sa le komangkanna boka kgoši;
Ge e le la'go lerato motsikiditlo le sa ntsikiditla ka wa maloba;
Ke a tseba phošo ke phošitše, fela nako mphe ya go phošolla;
Mphe nako re tsošološe tša maloba, tša maabane re di latše.

Hle mphe nako ke be ke sa itire
Ge ke be ke iphetošitše kgotho ke le motho!
Ke be ke sa itire, bošemane mogopolong bo be bo ntšwahletše;
Ke be ke sa itire, mogofe o be o nkgogotše ke go botše;
Ke be ke sa itire, ke be ke gamotše tša gore monna ke thaka-
Ke be ke sa itire, ke be ke kwele go thwe a monna makako-

Hle nneele meetse diatleng, ke be ke gakanegile ke nwele a legakwa!
Kaka Morwamotho ga makgolo a šupago ntebalele o lebale, motho 'a ka;
A re tšee taba ka selepe re reme e sa tapunya bjalo ka phogwana' ngwana;
A re dule fase molepo taba re šoge manaba a se nabe ka tša rena;
Hle a re dule tlase re budulele mollo woo o bego o timile!

Mphe nako tshehlana' Balobedu balobathaba!
Mphe nako re tsošološe dikwi di se hwelele re dikwa;
Ke ra tšona tšela tša go re tsošetša a lerato malopo;
Ke ra tšona tšela tša go re tsebiša lerato re sa tsebane;
Hle mphe nako kgadi 'a Banareng!

GIVE ME A CHANCE!

Pheladi, the absolute ruler in my heart, please give me a chance!
Give me a chance, my heart still belongs to you like in the past.
You are still roaming in my heart, like a king you're still a supreme ruler;
The tingle of your love still tickles as that of the past.
I know that I wronged you but afford me a chance to correct my wrongdoings;
Give me a chance to resurrect our past, and forget about yesterday.

Please, give me a chance I was not myself
When I was behaving like a male dog while I'm a human!
I was not myself, my mind was infiltrated by boyhood;
I was not myself, truly I was captured by peer-pressure;
I was not myself, I was misadvised that a man is a pumpkin vine-
I was not myself, I heard a saying which says a man's porridge heaps-

Please forgive me, I was suffering from dilemma due to confusion;
Like the Son of God, forgive me seventy times seven times, my love;
Let's destroy this complication while it's still soft like a fontanelle of an infant;
Let's settle down and resolve this issue to avoid gossips by our enemies;

Please, let's settle down and rekindle the dying spark of our love!

Give me a chance my light skinned girl from Balobedu tribe!
Give me a chance to resurrect our feelings before they disappear for good;
Feelings which awakened our spirits of love;
Feelings which inaugurated us to love while we were strangers.
Please give me a chance, the daughter of Banareng!

MOŠOMO WO

Mošomo wona ka dintaka re a bona,
Kaka thakadu o swere o sa saswe o a šoma;
Fela wo mošomo o a mmakatša ge nka go botša;
Fela wo mošomo ka bogolo ka megolo o a re boa;
Le ge o šoma wa Ramaatla wa, "tswalang le ate..."
Fela nnete re ka se go botše maaka.

Selemo, Marega madibeng o boa ntshe o ipošeletša;
Ke Lehlabula, ke Seruthwana sa mahlwaana se se;
Nke mmantepa lefaseng o nnoši.
Nke matutu o tshotshoma o nnoši.
Na ge o ka gomela o tla gagolwa ke eng?

Nywaga e re o kgarebjana ye nanana.
Eupša mošomotlou wa gago o arogile;
Eupša mošomong wo o kadijela ya mahlwaadibona;
Digatlelane o gatletše ntle le go lewa ke dihlong;
Mola mahlong a setšhaba o leša dihlong.
Ngwagola e be ba le tlhano, molengwaga šebao,
Ba tsheletše go monwana wa bo selela.

Batala ba lekile go o sokolla ba go tshepile,
Ya ba go nošetša leswika ka meetse...
Ba ipea dipelotšhwaana ka la gore tsebe ba tseba
E se na sekhuromelo gomme monatsebe o kwele,
Kgane ya bago gona o ntšhang ka ga tšhwene;
Ba go bea fase ka polelo, eupša mmolelo
Wa ba gaša ka wa mae a go bola.
A ka nnete ke gona ge o gana go gopotšwa nnete?

Mmamotswadi ka go lela a go letše o kwaletše;
Mmamotswadi ke motswadi go tswetše wena;
Wa'go mošomo o mmipetše sepotata ke go botše;
Phori mahlong o mo gaša mehla ye;
Maloba o rile mošomo Polokwane;
Kgane mošomo ke go boa o beputše;
Maabane wa re letogwana Mokopane;
Fela wa re tlaba o boa o kukile mpua;
Lehono o re mašemo Mamelodi 'a Tshwane;
Re tla re ke dipitsi ka mebala re bona.

THIS LABOUR

With our eyes we can see your toil;
Like an Aardvark you're soberly toiling.
But as an individual, truly speaking I'm forever surprised by this toil;
But as elders we are entirely fed up of this toil;
Even though you are toiling God's mandate of "be fruitful…"
But truly we cannot lie to you.

Summer, Winter you give birth repeatedly;
Whether is autumn or Spring, there is an infant.
It seems like you are the only woman in the world.
It seems like you are the only one with perspiring breast milk.
What will maul you if you abandon that toil?

Your age states that you are a mere young girl.
But your enormous toil states otherwise;
But on your toil you are an experienced veteran.
You have birthed consecutively without a shame;
While you are a shame in the eyes of the public.
Last year they were five, this year there they are,
They have crossed to the seventh finger.

Elders tried to show you sense with trust,
But all their attempts failed dismally.
They had hopes that since an ear
Doesn't have a lid, then you have heard them;
Their attempt failed since you escalated your toil.
They tried you with a sensible talk, but you replied
By throwing spoiled eggs on their face.
Are you now indeed disputing to be reminded the truth?

Your mother who nurtured you is tired of raising;
Your mother is a parent while you are the one who birthed.
Truly speaking she's entirely bloated from your toil.
You are always lying to her.
The other day you told her of a job in Polokwane;
But that job was to come back with an infant on your back.
Yesterday you told her about a temporary job in Mokopane;
But we were shocked when you came back carrying an infant.
Today you are talking about employment in Mamelodi.
We will believe by seeing.

MOENG KA GEŠO

A re šwahlela re sa itlomoka ka tša lefaseng.
A re šwahlela šebešebe e rena ka lapeng.
A re khukhunetša re nabile maoto ka bophelo.
A re khukhunetša re sa khukhuna le tša bophelo

A goroga le go ikgata mehlala re hlaletše,
Mehlala a ikgata a thothile, hlogo ye ntsho ra bolawa,
Mehlala a ikgata a rwaleletše, a re lobišitše.
Wa madi a rena a tloga naye godimo a lebeletše,
Wa madi a rena a tingwa gosasa re kgohlotše.
Bja monetho phelo a gogola le monkgo.
Bja monetho phelo a kga ka nkgo.

A re bakela sebabo, a re hlolela sengalo,
Manyami a re kgotholela, lemyemyelo a amoga,
Bophelo a re babišetša, bohloko a bjala pelong.
Mahlodi ra kgothola boka ya medupi.
Sello sa hloka segotlane, sa hloka putswa,
Ya ba semphetekegofete ya go se kgitla.

Melomo ra šala re thibile ka seatla a fulere,
Mantšu ra šala re sena kaka semuma,
Kamogelo ra gana etšwe phenyo re tšere.

Yo moeng le ge re mo tšhaba ke wa setšhaba,
Yo moeng ke wa bajaboloko ke wa bajabalahla.
Lehono o etile ka gešo, bosasa o eta ka geno.

A VISITOR AT MY HOMESTEAD

He attacked us while we were still enjoying earthly sweetness;
He attacked us while peace was reigning at home;
He stalked us while we were relaxed with our livelihood;
He stalked us while we were creeping with livelihood matters.

He arrived and returned back while we were observing.
He took from us before going back, destroying us entirely;
He carried what's ours before going back, losing ours wholly.
One from our bloodline was taken along with him lifeless;
One from our bloodline was deprived another day while we were gazing.
The life of my sibling was taken by him clearly.
The life of my sibling was drawn with a water-pitcher by him.

He caused us an itch, he brought us about a bruise;
He dumped sorrows on us, then took our smiles away.
Our lives were bittered, pain was sown in our hearts;
Like a long continued rainfall our tears fell.
There was no an elder or a child when coming to lamentation;
We all competed with a lament.

We were left shocked while the visitor was gone;
Like people with mutism we were left speechless.
We refused to accept, although we took the defeat.

Even though we fear this visitor, he is for the people.
This visitor visits poor people and rich people alike.
Today he visited my homestead, tomorrow he will visit yours.

LE HLANKELA MANG?

Le hlankela mang?
Ka gore šefao le hlwela go hlankela le sa hlahlarege.
Bošego mosegare le hlankišwa ke go hlankela;
Mohlankedi ke sa hlahlathe o gona le a hlankela.
Bjalo, le hlankela mang?

Bohlankedi bja lena bo a re tlhakiša, ke le tsebiše;
Bohlankedi bja lena bo re hlohloniša ka bophelo;
Go dulela go hlankela ga lena go re bilošetša bophelo;
Ka mešego yohle, ka oto le tee re a hlwa ra lala.

Le hlankela mang?
Ka gore setšhaba se a itšhatšhara e le didirwa ke lena;
Megokgo se kgothola boka segotlane le bona.
Batiišamolao tlase le tletlolo ke sa bona go tsongwana le lena;
Batiišamolao le nkgišetšana nabo mahwafa ka dibetša le itlamile;
Maanomabe e le go tšhaba go lebana le tsogo la molao le letile;
Kgangkgolo e le go boifa go lebanwa ke diheketšhipi tša ntloleswiswi.

Ntle le dihlong, dilešadihlong setšhabeng le a dira;
Sekgaphamamila, putswa theto le phaya dihlong le tonkutše;
Thoto tša batho la thotha botho le itebaditše;
Mantho setšhošwane la fapantšha le pula nke le madira.
Na motswadi le tswetšwe ke ofe ge le ilalo le hwile matswalo?
Na le reng ka melao ye lesome ya ngwalo la masomepedi la Ekisodi?

Mpotšeng, le hlankela mang?
Ntomeng tsebe ka nnete ke kweng.
Ge e le Ramaatla ke gana nnang!
Tša lena tiro ke tša Raleswiswi ke le botšeng!.
Ya lena mediro ke ya mmušo wa leswiswi, ntshepeng!

WHO ARE YOU SERVING?

Who are you serving?
Because there you are, always serving without hesitation;
Day and night you are enslaved by serving.
Truly speaking there's a master you are serving.
Thus, who are you serving?

Be notified that we are suffering due to your serving ways;
Our lives are itchy because of your serving ways.
Your lives of forever serving is destroying our lives.
Day and night we are suffering daily.

Who are you serving?
Because people are suffering due to your doings;
Like a toddler they are dropping tears while you are watching.
Law enforcers go up and down searching for you;
Armed, you go toe to toe with law enforcers.
Badly intending to avoid facing the forever waiting might of the law;
Mainly battling with a fear of facing prison steel gates.

Without any shame you are doing shameful deeds to people.
You rape children and elders without any shame;
Without showing humanity, you steal people's properties;
Like evil soldiers you murder people as if they are ants.
Which parent gave birth to soulless people like you?
What do you say about Ten Commandments in the book of Exodus twenty?

Tell me, who are you serving?
Whisper in my ear; let me hear the truth;

Because I know that you are not serving The Mighty One;
Your deeds are that of Satan, I'm telling you!
Your doings are that of the dark world, trust me!

Simbarashe Andrew Kashiri (Zimbabwe): Poems in chiShona

Mwari tirangarireiwo

Tinonofamba nzira nenzendo dzinorema
Nedzimwe nguva tinoneta, hatina simba
Tiratidzeiwo kubata kwenyu, zvinorema
Pfungwa dzedu hadzingazvigone ...

Sango racho rizere minzwa nezvikara
Zuva rinopisa, pasina mvura
Taisa muteuro kwamuri tenzi
Tirangarirei, tiri vana venyu ...

Nzizi dzacho hadziyambukiki
Makomo acho matero- haakwiriki
Kwese kwataenda, zvimhingaidzo –
Ishe tiri vana venyu, tipeiwo zano ...

Vamwe vaive mugomba reshumba
Vamwewo ndivo vakakandwa mumoto
Vamwe vakarwisaniswa nendimba-ndimba
Vamwewo vakagurwa musoro...

Hamungatadze kutinunura
Ndimi mega mungatotibatsira
Tiri nherera dzenyu sezvandareva
Tibatsireiwo sezvamakaita vamwe ...

God remember us

We traverse difficult journeys and paths
At times we get weary, we are weak
Show us your might, we are heavy laden
We can't reason our way out – our minds cannot handle it ...

The wilderness is thorny and full of deadly creatures
The sun is blazing hot, and we are thirsty
We've sent a prayer to you, dear God
Remember us, we are your children ...

The rivers are too treacherous to cross
The mountains are too steep and unclimbable
Everywhere we go we're facing challenges
God, we are your children
Give us a solution...

There are some who were thrown in a lions den
Some were thrown in blazing hot furnaces
Some were called to fight giants
And others had their heads chopped off ...

You can't fail to deliver us
You're the only one who can save us
We're your orphans, as mentioned before
Please help us, as you've helped others before ...

Inini ndaikuda ...

Pandakatanga kukuona mwana iwewe
Moyo wanga wakafara segwenga
Rasangana nemvura kekutanga
Wakanyemwerera ndikati, ndamuwana wangu.
Takazozivana nekufamba kwemwaka,
Rudo rwuchipisa, pasina zvinonetsa
Pane hapo zvakazopindira zvakaipa
Ukatanga kundidadira, ndisisaite
Asi ndinoti kwauri mwanasikana
Ini ndaikuda nehuipi hwako hwese
Nekuti hakuna munhu pasi rese rino
Asina chipomerwa chero pakavhiringidzika.
Ndaikupa rudo, rwemandorokwati
Ndichikuzora mafuta, wapedza kugeza
Ndaikujuma netwunonaka usingafungire
Ndichimbozevezera munzeve dzako, wakandibatirira...
Zvino wakawana mumwe, handichakuitire
Wavekuti handina pfuma, hauone zambuko
Waiti uchava neni nekusingaperi
Zvino kasingaperi, kakazopera.
Ndinozvitambira hangu, ndizvo zvinoita hupenyu
Dai munhu asiri munhu pamwe takazoenda mberi.
Ufambe zvakanaka, handina daka newe
Nguva ndiyo yakatisanganisa, asi zvakazoguma
Tichasangana hedu, ndofunga kudenga
Nekuti zvepasirino zvokwadi zvakakona
Chaive chishuvo changu, tirambe tichidanana
Asi chero vemagitare vanotaura wani:
Panozosvika nguva iyo, mhanzi painomira...

Personally, I loved you ...

When I first saw you, young lady
My heart was elated like a desert
Receiving rain for the first time
You smiled and I thought "she's the one
Then we got acquainted as the seasons passed
Our love burned bright, we had no issues
Until bad things reared their ugly heads
And I was no longer good enough for you
But I say to you, young lady
I truly loved you, despite your faults
Because there's no-one under the heavens
Who is without fault or blemish ....
I gave you true love, wholeheartedly
I'd lotion up your skin, after a bath
And surprise you with unexpected gifts, ever so often
And lovingly whisper in your ear, when we were joined in love ...
Because you've found someone else, I'm no longer worthy
I'm too poor for you, you don't see a future
Yet you said you'd be with me forever
Yet forever somehow diminished ...
I accept though, it's part of life
If people weren't human, we could have progressed
I hope your journey is good, I hold no grudges
Time had joined us, but everything came to an end
We'll meet again, maybe in heaven
Because clearly, on this plane our love failed
It was my wish that we'd stay in love
But even those who play music agree:

There has to be a time when the music stops...

Abdullatif Eberhard Khalid (Uganda): Poems in Gikuyu and Kiswahili

THIINI WA GŨTŨRŨRŨ

Aarî mũciî wa gũtũrũrũ
Rũmũ rwake rwonagîrîra mũhîrîga wa boardwalk
Gũtũrũrũ gwakoragwo gwîcîrîte
Thiga wera
Mũno wendo wa mahiu
Rî ũtũkũ rîa gũtũgũrũ—ndîa ũgîkũ
Na irîa rîa rũthingo rîkũmbũka mahiũ,
Ũga wakwa ũkaragwo ta maîta makũũmbũkaga.

Ũtukũ ũmwe ngîkũrîa, agîcoka kũgũa mũîrîa
Agîtũũra mũhîrîga wa kîrîra
Agîthîna na ngũî nîo makũrîa mũgũnda
Mwerũ wakwa ũkũrugîra gwîtũkũ
Ũgîthîkîra mîgũrũ ya mahiũ
Na mwerũ ũgîcaria mũgîrîri wake
Mahiũ matagataga ta meciria ya nduma
Makũhîa na kũhîa
Makîmũkîra mũno

Akainîrîrio
Ndarehîrwo
Ata ũtukũ ũkînyîtîre na ngwenda kũga
Ndareka kũmenyera mũgîrîri wa mwerũ na ngũî
Ũrîa makũheaga tha na ũrîa meciria yao yakũmenyera

THE BEACH

She was staying at the beach.
Her room looked out over the boardwalk.
The beach was peaceful.
White sand.
Clear blue water.
The sun was warm — not too hot.
And when the sunlight touched the water,
The reflection looked like sparkling diamonds.
One night after dinner, she went to sit on a bench.
She sat by the walkway.
She faced the ocean and watched the waves.
The moon shone brightly in the night
Lighting up the tops of the waves.
And the moon seemed to be moving with the water.
The waves danced like thoughts in a dream —
Rising and falling,
Growing stronger and stronger.
She was enchanted.
She couldn't look away.
Even when it got late and she needed to go,
She stayed, watching the moon and the waves,
How they shared a secret rhythm together,
Like they were calling her into their mystery.

MALAIKA DHIDI YA SHETANI

Malaika na shetani wanaishi ndani yetu,
Wote wanapigana kuunda hali yao ya utu,
Yule anayeshinda hutawala akili na moyo,
Na yule mwingine hutulia, kisha hutoweka kwa woga.
Shetani huonyesha dunia ya udanganyifu,
Ambako kila kitu huonekana chema na cha kuvutia mno,
Hutuletea vishawishi vya kupendeza,
Na kutupeleka kwenye maovu na maangamizi bila huruma.
Shetani huruhusu tufanye lolote kwa raha ya muda,
Na hupoteza nguvu zetu kwa mambo yasiyo na faida,
Huchukua udhibiti wa hisia zetu zote,
Na kutuchochea tufanye dhambi nzito na mbaya mno.
Malaika huonyesha ukweli wa maisha yetu,
Maisha yaliyojaa furaha na majaribu pia,
Hutufundisha kudhibiti hisia zetu kwa hekima,
Na kushinda kelele za raha zenye hila na tamaa.
Malaika haturuhusu tufanye uovu kwa makusudi,
Kwa kuwa yeye hutaka tuungane na asili ya kiungu,
Hutuongoza kutembea njia ngumu na sahihi,
Ili tuache alama ya kudumu na ya maana duniani.
Basi, nani atatawala roho zetu kweli?
Nani atakuwa na nafasi kuu na ya pekee?
Atakuwa ni yule tunayempa nguvu zaidi,
Na katika mipango yake, tutapenda kuishi na kudumu ndani.

ANGEL VS DEMON

Angel and demon both resides in us,
They both fight to create their type of atoms,
The one who wins, rules over our head and heart,
And the other one, sits silent and moves apart.

Demon shows us the illusionary world,
Where everything seems beautifully impearled,
He gives us enticing temptations,
And leads us to moral degradation.

Demon allows us to do anything for temporary pleasure,
And wastes all our energy in futile endeavor,
He takes control of all our senses,
And provokes us to do heinous offences.

Angel shows us the real picture of our life,
Which is a web of happiness and strife,
He teaches us how to handle different emotions,
And how to beat delightful commotions.

Angel doesn't allow us to do mischievous things,
As He tries to establish our divine link,
He guides us to tread on the difficult track,
So that we could leave our profound impact.

So, who will take control over our soul?
Who will play the most important role?
He will be the one, to whom we nourishes the most,
And in whose plans, we want to get engrossed.

Viti vitupu—

Matador asema kwa moto,
maono yamemeza kimya.

Empty chairs remain—
the Matador speaks with fire,
visions drown silence.

Jeshi Bila Wanajeshi.

Jeshi lisilo na wanajeshi,
ni mavumbi yakipigana na upepo—
hakuna mwelekeo, ni machafuko,
uovu unacheza kwenye kimbunga.
Lakini tukisimama pamoja,
tunapigana kulinda ardhi yetu.
Bila umoja, tutapotea,
tutaachwa tupu kama jangwa lenye kiu.
Ndani ya kuta hizi kuna maana,
ya kuilinda dhidi ya dhoruba.
Vita siyo uovu kila wakati—
wakati mwingine ndiyo wokovu wa roho.
Upepo hujaribu kututenganisha,
vivuli huvaa tabasamu bandia.
Ukikataa kupigana,
majaribu yatakumeza ukiwa hai.
Watu usiowajua hujitokeza,
wakiwa na tamaa zilizofichwa.
Na usipoinua ngao yako,
unaacha moyo wangu kuvunjika.
Samahani haitoshi,
ukiniacha na maumivu moyoni.
Kama unajali, ungesimama kupigana—
usingeacha hisia ziangamie.
Majaribu huingia taratibu,
yakipeperusha wageni kwenye nafasi yako.
Watu huanguka kwenye tamaa,
sio kwa sababu ya nguvu, bali udhaifu wao.
Kwa sababu nguvu si kelele za "mimi ni alpha,"
ni kupigana vita visivyoonekana.

Ni mapambano ya ndani ya roho
yanayoamua sisi ni akina nani.

Army Without Soldiers

An army without soldiers
is just dust clashing in the wind—
no purpose, only chaos,
evil swirling in the whirlwind.
But when we stand as one,
we fight to guard our space.
Without unity, it's lost,
left empty like a desert's face.
Within these walls lies meaning,
worth sparing from the storm.
War isn't always evil—
sometimes it's how we're formed.
The wind tries to pull us apart,
with shadows wearing smiles.
If you don't stand and fight,
temptation feeds on your denial.
Unfamiliar faces draw near,
with desires sharp and sly.
And if you hesitate to battle,
you let our bond die.
Sorry won't be enough
when your silence brings me pain.
If you cared, you'd have fought—
not watched it slip like rain.
Temptation creeps in softly,
blows strangers into your place.

People cheat, not from power,
but from weakness they can't face.
Because strength isn't shouting "alpha,"
it's fighting what eyes can't see—
the silent wars within us
that decide who we will be.

WEWE!

Ulinizungumza kwa njia
ambayo hakuna mwingine aliwahi kunizungumzia —
na kwa kufanya hivyo,
uliguza sehemu za moyo wangu
nilizodhani zimekufa kitambo.
Ilinitia hofu, kwa kweli.
Wazo kwamba huenda nisiishi vya kutosha
kukionyesha kina cha upendo wangu kwako,
kukutoa sadaka hii kamili— bila woga, bila kujizuia.
Mara nyingi nilisimama pembeni mwa wazo hilo:
Je, nisubiri ufungue mlango?
Au niondoke kwa ajili ya amani yangu mwenyewe?
Ulihitajika kuniruhusu niingie — au uniache niende.
Lakini hata hivyo — hata kama usingewahi chagua —
kuna jambo moja nililolijua kwa uhakika.
Bado ningekupenda. Katika maisha haya. Katika yajayo.
Katika kila hali ya wakati inayoweza kuwepo.
Ulikuwa, na utabaki milele,
upendo wangu wa mwisho — na wa milele.

YOU!

You spoke to me in a way no one ever had —
and in doing so, you touched parts of me
I thought had long since died.
It scared me, honestly.
The idea that I might never live long enough
to show you the full depth of my love,
to offer it to you completely, without fear or holding back.

I often stood at the edge of that thought:
should I wait for you to open the door,
or should I walk away for my own peace?
You needed to either let me in or let me go.

But even then — even if you never made the choice —
I knew one thing with certainty.

I would still love you. In this life. In the next.
In every version of time that could possibly exist.

You were, and always will be,
my last and forever love.

William Khalipwina Mpina (Malawi): Poems in chiChewa

Sindili Chimodzimodzi

Mantha ochititsa mantha
Msuzi wa misozi udonthera
Pa thanthwe la nkhawa
Wako mpando uli phuthi, kudikira
Kuyesa udzabweranso
Kulephera kutakataka
Kugwiragwira kupondaponda
Zako zithunzi
Zikusekelera ndikaziyang'ana
Yanga nkhope ili nyontcholi
Umboni woti mbebe wachikondi udalipo ndithu
Umasiyewu wandionetsa maliseche anjoka
Kuyesayesa kuthamangathamanga kuti ndizitolere
Ayi ndithu. Sindili chimodzimodzi popanda iwe.
Tikamati "Ife" kapena "uje ndi ujeni"
Ndi mtendere wokhutuka umene uja
Ndatsala ndekha "ine," kukwapuka ndi chisanu
Pamene dziko lidakagudumuka, osandilabadira.

I am Not the Same

Fear that scares fear
A stream of tears dripping
On the rock of burden
Your chair is empty, waiting
Thinking you will come back
I am failing to fend for myself
For I am trying, and trying
Your pictures
Laugh at me when I look at them
My face is so sad
A proof that there was warm love
Death has shown me the true meaning of survival
I am trying, but I am failing
No, of course. I'm not the same without you.
Saying "We" is a lie, "Mr and Mrs,"
Is an overflowing peace
I'm left with "me," shivering with cold
While the world keeps spinning, not caring.

Thambo la Mvula Likadza

Thambo la mvula likadza
Thambo lokhuthala ndi madzi
Osachita nalo mantha
Ako malingaliro akhale pa kaduwa
Aka kaduwa komwe kadafotaka
Dontho la mvula likupatse chimwemwe
Likhale nyimbo yoimbidwa kachetechete
Nyimbo yokondwelera moyo
Ena akalira, kukubwera namondwe!
Iwe udziti, kukubwera madzi
Muthambolo, upenyemo moyo
Mabingu akalira ngati ng'oma
Kutali uko, kulengeza za chilengedwe
Wako mtima uchite mweetu
Uko ndiko kulekana
Nacho chilimwe
Dzinja lidze
Mvula igwe
Pansi panyowe
Kaya ndi namondwe
Kaya tilira mayi wawaye
Kuseliko kuli zabwino zake!

When the Rain Cloud Comes

When the rain cloud comes
A cloud, thick with water
Fear not
Let your thoughts be on the flower
The flower that has withered
Let a drop of rain give you joy
Let it be a song sung quietly
A song that rejoices life
When they see a storm
You must see water
In that rain cloud, you must see life
When the thunder beats like a drum
Far away, announcing the beauty of nature
Let your heart smile
At the signal of separation
There goes summer
Let autumn come
Let the rain fall
Let it wet the ground
Whether it is a storm
Whether we will cry
Something good shall always come!

Ifésinàchi Nwàdiké (Nigeria): Poems in Igbo

Haiku Anọ Maka Nnem

Nne m
Ị chetara ụzọ ahụ
Ebe anyị túfùrù ụbụrụ ịsị anyị?

II
Nne m
Amụ anyị ejughi zi ha afọ
Ị here mégbuo abalị a mụrụ anyị

III
Nne m
Biko weta mkpịsị edemede ọbara ọbara ahụ
Oge eruola ịgụ ozu anyị ọnụ ọzọ

IV
Nne m
A gwara m gi na ara dị iché iché
A hụrụ m ótù ụzọ tàà

Four Haikus for Dear Mother

Dear mother
Do you still recall the junction
Where we lost our senses?

II

Dear mother
They're no longer content with small penises
Shame to our birth nights
III

Dear mother
Please get the bloody marker, it's time
To count our dead again

IV

Dear mother
I told you that madness has many shades
I saw one today

Haiku Ano Maka Nwam

Nwa m, Rome
Dara n'ófù ụbọchị
Sité na nkàtà ụmụ ya

II

Ányánwụ
Na àdà na owulo
Wụrụ ọnwa, nwa m

III

Nwa m, zochaa échichè gị
N'ime àkpà óbi gị
Ụwa wụ onye Ịsị Ojịị

IV

Weré irè gị
Gụọ ézè gị ọnụ, nwa m
Ntị gị i nwere nti

Four Haikus for Dear Son

Son, Rome fell by the
conspiracy of patriots, bridle your tongue
your cheeks have ears

II

Even the sun sets
at noon, the world trudges on
son, be the moon

III

Hide your thoughts
in the parrot of your soul, son
the world is a Blackman

IV

Learn to laugh in syllables
like a hypocrite concealing his hate
for his very jester, son

Vihje Ben Nkhunga (Malawi): Poem in chiChewa

IMFA YA MAYI
(dedicated to my late mother Emily Leah Namande Nkhunga)

Kupita kwa mayi,
N'chipasupasu.
Kupita kwa mayi,
Khomo ndi bwinja.

MAMA'S DEMISE

A mother's last breath
is the strike of a hurricane.
Mama's final eyes' closure
is absolute desolation.

Saratu Muhammad Adamu (Nigeria): Poems in Hausa

KEWAR MASOYI

Ya me warkar da zuciyata,
Ya me warkar da ruhina,
Me yasa kake damun mafarkina?
Kai ne madubin idaniya ta.
Kyakkyawar fuskarka takan yiman gizo.
Zuciyata ta daɗe tana begenka.

Kai kaɗai zuciyata take marari.
Muryarka tana yaye min damuwa ta.
Ina jin kusancinka a tattare dani.
Wannan zuciyar me rauni tana kewarka.
Kaunarka ta dabaibaye ni tamkar a kurkuku.

Ya kai mafarkin raina,
Ka saurari masoyiya mai kaunarka.
Zuciyarta na shaukinka,
Tana kwaɗayin kyautatawarka,
Tana kwaɗayin kulawarka da kusancinka.
Wannan masoyiya tana ƙara neman aminicewar soyayyarka.

LONGING

O, healer of my heart,
O, healer of my soul,
Why do you linger in my dreams?
When I shut my eyes, you are all I see -
Your radiant face haunts my every thought.
Can't you hear the cries of my yearning heart?

You are the only one it craves.
Your voice soothes my deepest sorrows,
And I feel your presence enveloping me.
This fragile heart aches for you;
You hold me captive
With your boundless love and compassion.

O, man of my dreams,
Listen to this prisoner of your affection.
This heart longs for your embrace,
It longs for your kindness,
And aches for your caring touch.
This prisoner yearns for freedom that only your love can grant.

MACE

Ita wata halitta ce,
Mai cike da tausayi, rauni, zumunci, da soyayya.
Zuciyarta ƙofa ɗaya ce da ita.
Haƙiƙa mutum ɗaya take mallakawa mukullinta.
Babu abinda ya kaita daɗi idan an fahimceta.
Ba'a mata dole a soyayya.
Bata tauna ɗan taura biyu a bakinta.
Takan so bawa ta ƙyale sarki.
Tabbas haka zuciyar mace take.
Amman tana da wani halin na daban.
Wanda ko shaiɗan yana jin tsoranta
Ɗafinta yafi na maciji illa.
Sharrinta yakan tashi daula guda.
Ya tarwatsa gidaje da zumunci.
Shaiɗan yakan ja da baya idan tayi alwashin ɗaukar fansa.
Takan maida sarki duk matsayin shi tamkar bawa.
Takan maida malami ya rausaya a gabanta.
Takan maida attajiri yazo maroƙi a gurinta.
Duk wani mai matsayi: talaka, attajiri, sarki, malami, ko ƙasƙantacce,
Shi dai burinsa ya mallake ta.
Mace tafi gwal tsada da daraja.
Mai hikimar fahimtar mace, zai dawwama a cikin annashuwa da salama.

WOMAN

A complex being she is,
Full of compassion, hurt, love, and tenderness.
Her heart beats for one alone, a key to a single lock.
Indeed, one person holds this key;
Nothing brings her joy if she's misunderstood.
She won't be forced into love;
She rejects duality in her heart.
She desires to be cherished, not commanded;
Her heart beats for devotion, not dominance.
Yet, she possesses a quality that even Satan fears,
Her venom is more potent than a snake's.
Evil can rise in an instant,
Destroying homes and relationships.
Satan retreats when she decides to take revenge;
She humbles a king, making him her servant.
She softens a scholar's heart, compelling him to plead before her;
She can make a wealthy person beg for her mercy.
Every individual, regardless of status - poor, rich, king, scholar, or noble -
Desires to possess her; she's more precious than treasure.
Whoever wins her heart finds joy; whether wise or not, her love is a treasure.

Yawo Baba (Togo): Poems in Ewe

DZUDZƆ ƲƆNUDƆDRƆ

Ame geɖe le abe bli wowo ene, wole dzoxɔxɔ me eye wokpɔa dzidzɔ
Wonye amesiwowɔa nusi mehiã o ɣesiaɣi
Ʋɔnudɔdrɔ si dzi wometsu ati ɖo enye wofe nuɖuɖu
Zi geɖe la, dzidzɔ alo vevesese nɔa te ɖe wò ŋutɔ wò nukpɔsusu le agbe ŋu dzi
Ke hã, kuxiwo kple nuteɖeamedziwo nɔa míafe dzi me
Ke hã, míetsɔanya kple nuteɖeamedzi ɖe asi
Le míafe dzime ɖe amesiwo metsɔa ɖeke le eme na mí gõ hã o ŋu

STOP JUDGING

Most of people are like popcorn, hot and thrilled
and who always run up on unnecessary show
Judging sans, hard-hitting reason is their foodstuff
Joy or pain often depends on your own perception of life
However, we carry issue and stress in our hearts
against those who don't even pay attention to us

ŊUTIFAFA ƒEAMEDODOWO

Ele be makɔ nye ta me
Medi be manɔnukpɔkpɔ deto vavan aɖe si me fefe
dodzidzɔname aɖe le
Abe alesi wònɔnale ƒuta ene la
Se atsiaƒu ƒeʋeʋẽ le eɖokuiwo me
Xɔ dzeya le wò ŋutilãa ŋu
Se ƒutake si le afɔwo te eye
Kpɔ ɣe si le ɣe ɖum si tsyɔa atsiaƒu me tsi dzi
Drõekula menye, ẽ nyemadzudzɔ drõekuku o
Malõ agbe ƒe ka
Abe nuɖala ene mele nya vevie ɖam fifia
Na xexea ƒe dzogoe eneawo
Woléa nusiwo wotsɔ wɔa nu ɣaɣlawo la ɖe ʋɔtru si le ʋuʋum la megbe
Xexeame galemɔ kpɔm na ŋutifafa
Ekem wɔ ɖekakpli mí aɖu Ablɔɖeha la ƒe azã
Abe ƒuƒoƒo ene la, mina míatu ɣletinyigba sesẽ aɖe
Ɖe Nyateƒe,anukwareɖiɖi, nuteƒewɔwɔ kple ɖekawɔwɔ dzi
Azɔ kpɔ dzidzɔ eye nàdo ŋutifafa ƒe asigɛa

PEACE AMBASSADORS

I need to empty my head
I want to live an apocalyptic scene
Where there is an interesting performance
Like at the beach
Feel the smell of the ocean
Feel the salt air on the body
Feel the quicksands under legs and
See the dancing sun covering the sea water
Dreamer yes I'll not stop dreaming
I weave the twine of life
As a chef I'm cooking right now
A solid word-meal for the whole world
The secret ingredients are held behind the sliding door
The world is still looking forward for peace
Join us to celebrate the freedom party
As a group let's build a stronger planet
On truths, honesty, loyalty and unity
Now be happy and wear the peaceful ring

NYAWO ƒEAKUNYAWƆWƆ

Eklẽna abe sika ene le nyawo ƒe dzime
Hakpanya ƒe vivisese nye nu xɔ asi ŋutɔ
Hakpakpa ƒoanu kple agbenɔƴi
Ehea dzidzɔ kple susudeblibo yia afsiafi
Eye emegbe agbe yia edzi abe ƴletivi dzodzo aɖe ene
Mɔnukpɔkpɔ kagbegbee nye si wònye be nànɔ agbe ahakpɔ ema adze sii!
Hakpakpa abe kadodo ƒe dziŋɔli ene
Gbɔgbɔ, seselelãme, ŋusẽ kple ŋusẽ yɔe
Hakpakpa abe nyawo ƒe akunyawɔwɔ ene nana xexeame me nɔa agbe
Eye wòseaveve ɖe ame nu
Hakpanya,nusiwo katã li ƒe dzɔtsoƒe
Hakpanya zɔna kple amesiwo le teƒe vovovowo siwo lea dzi ɖe nu
Alo menyenenema o
Woah! Woah! Kɔnua ƒe Aƒetɔ le ƴeyiƴi kpui aɖe ko me ƒoa nu
Menye ɖeko wòɖi ya o ke eɖi ƒutsotsoe hã
Hakpakpa nyekesinɔnu dzadzɛ aɖe si wotsɔ ƒo ƒu hena susu ƒe akɔdzeanyi
Hakpakpa ƒehakpakpa, hakpanya egbea, hakpanya etsɔ, hakpanya tegbee hakpanyawo le afima zigbɔ zi geɖe zi gbɔ zi geɖe

THE MAGIC OF WORDS

It shines as well as gold in the heart of the words
Poetic vibe is trully sacred
POETRY pulsates with the lifetime
It brings hapiness and full reason everywhere
And then life goes on, such a shooting star
What a chance to be alive and realizing that!
Poetry as communication rainbow
It is full of breathing, emotions, energy and power
Poetry as magic of words, makes the world more vivid and sensitive
Poetry, source of all existence
Poetry walks with people on different places, who are interesting in it or not
Wow! Master of ceremony who without further ado blows
Not only like wind but also like sea wave
Poetry is a pure treasure needed for peace of mind
Poetry yesterday, poetry today, poetry tomorrow, poetry forever
Poetry is there again and again

AƒENƆ SI TSIAKOGO LA

Eƒe ta le veve sem
Eƒe dzi hã
Tamesusuwo lee dzoe
Eƒe tamesusuwo xɔa eƒe ɣeyiɣi
Esia nye nyavevie aɖe
Aƒemelã menye naneke nɛ o
Eye nuɖuɖu nye agba sesẽ ne eyama
Metsɔ ɖeke le naneke me o
Enɔ tsa ɖim le võwo me ŋkeke kple zã
Abe alesi wòle le nɔnɔmetata si ƒe didime nye akpa blibo dziŋɔ aɖe me ene
Ŋkuwo miia gake gbɔɖeme aɖeke meli o

THE LONELY

Her head is in pain
Her heart too
Thoughts kidnapped her
Thoughts steal her time
This is a critical point
Pet means nothing to her
And eating, a hard duty
She is not interested in anything
She has been cruising evils
Days and nigths
As in a horrible full-length feature film in high-definition
Eyes closed but no rest

Bala Abubakar Daddere (Nigeria): Poems in Hausa

Hausa Language	English Translation
Rayuwa	**Life**
Rayuwa wasan dara game	Life, a dice
Shagaltarwa take har dare ya doso until night falls	It engages one
Ga ta nan kamar birgimar hankaka coloured object	It is a double-
Kowa ya ga farin ta sees its white colour	Whoever

Wataran zai ga bakin ta day see its black colour	Will one
Haka ma take kamar taunan goruba a solid fruit	It is like chewing
Da laluba take kai ga makoshi to pass through the esophagus	It requires gentle chew
Rayuwa	Life
Kamar zuma take idan ta ba da gaba when in perfect shape	It is like honey
In ta ki lago sai ta zamo madachi turns upside down	But bitter when the table
Rayuwa	Life
Kamar tafiyar biri ce monkey's walk	It is like a
Da gudu da tsalle tsalle jumping	Runing and
Kuma da waiwaye da leke check and peeping	With sides
Rayuwa	Life
Kamar hanjin jimina take ostrich's intestine	Its like an
Akwai na chi the one to consume	There is
Akwai na zubarwa. one to discard.	And the

Rabo

Rabo Kamar bullar rana yake
sun rise
Idan ya yunkuro
rise
Tafin hannu ba ya masa kyaure
can't cover it's rays
Haka ma zancen yake
Idan kasuwa ta ki bawa
fails a man
Sai ya kasa barkonu
display pepper
Ache babu yaji.
complain of not being pepperish.

Fortune

Fortune is like

When it is set to

The palm

That's how it is
When business

He will

Others will

Bakuwar Tilas Stranger	The Inevitable
Ni dai al'amarin ki yana firgita ni trajectory	Your always drives me to dolour
Wani sa'in ya kan bani tausayi makes me emphatic	Sometimes it
Ya sa ni chikin tuntuni da bege to be sober	Making me
Yadda kike bin umurni babu cheto rules without intercession	The way you observe
Babu nawa a gare ki ko da kika even within the tinkle of an eye	No delay in your action
Ko gida a ke, ko a daji bush	At home or in the
Ko dare ne, ko da rana day time	At night or in the
A sama bawa ya ke ko a rami inside a ditch	In the sky or
Kin dau da chikin uwar sa a baby inside the womb	You claim
Kin dau uwa da uba kin bar marayu ba madafa parent and leave orphans to uncertainty	You claim
Mai akwai ko de da babu the have not	Haves and
Idan ajalin sa ya zo babu kauna nature calls there is no mercy	When
Gargadi ki ke mai bayar da soro admonition scares one	Your

Yayin da ki ka zo bin umurni	When it is time to observe the will
Babu ruwan ki da masayi na bawa;	You don't mind one's position
Shagalalle ne ko dai nasasse	Whether a deviant or devotee
Allah ya sa mu chika da kyau	May we transit in good fate
Yanzun ne ko anjima	Whether now or later
Ki sa me mu chikin masu karban umurni	So that you meet us as righteous beings
Da takawa da imani da bin tafarki.	With chastity, faith and righteousness.

Mai Hasada / Envious

Mai Hasada	The
Envious	
Mai hasada ya na shan wuya dilemma	The envious is in
Domin da gilli chikin zuciya loaded with black clot	His heart is
Ba shi da alheri sai tarin tsiya except distraction	He has no plans
Mai hasada uban yan harsaniya envious, master of evil	The
Kamar dan akuya ya ke mai aikin tsiya goat the chief deviant	He is like a
Ya tunkushi uba, ya tura wa uwa jijiya and inserts its gbola into its mother	Who hits its father
Mai hasada envious	The
A kafe yake kullun babu harkar gaba static without progress	He is always
Domin zuciyar sa chike take da annakiya his heart is loaded with filth	Because
Mai hasada ya na da halin dan uba the traits of a half-brother	The envious has
Bai da aiki sai chin dunduniya is to hit his brother's foot	Whose pleasure
Batun sa sharri ne kullun safiya are always distracting	His words

Mai hasada	The envious
Da za ka yarda da Rabbana	If only you trust God
Mai bayar da arziki ga bawa ta ko ina	That gives wealth to whoever He wishes
Da rayuwa ta tafi daidai ba shan wuya.	Life would have been prestine without regret.

Gaskiya Dokin Karfe

Truth, the Iron Horse

Gaskiya dokin Karfe,	Truth the iron horse
kowa in ya hau bazai yi nadama ba	Whoever rides will not regret
Rabo in ya rantse	When fortune comes around
Hasada bazai yi tasiri ba	Envy will not find a place
Agola da tinkaho	No matter the place of an adopted one
Ba zai zamo da ba	He can't be a biological son
Tuwon kishiya	An opponent's meal
Sai dai achi ba domin dadi ba	Is eaten not for its taste
Kirge ya bata	The statistic is mixed up

Tunda biyar biyu ya kasa yin goma	Since two fives can't make ten
Zancen na mai hikima ne	This is for those with wisdom
Kamar kukan kurciya yake	Like a bird's melody
Sai mai hankali yake ganewa.	Only the stable mind decodes

Aryan Kaganof (South Africa): Poems in Afrikaans

Is die esel 'n donkie?

My weefsel kraak.

Ek voel soos alles wat ek sê, kak is.

Alles wat in my gat moet gebeur, gebeur êrens anders.

In my esel gebeur niks nie.

Dit is ek wat die kook doen.

Dit gaan in en dit gaan af, maar niks kom uit nie.

Ek word albei 'n gewer en nemer van stront.

Ek wonder of daar baie mans soos hierdie in Suid-Afrika is?

Is the ass a donkey?

My tissue is cracking.

I feel like everything I say is shit.

Everything that should happen in my ass is happening somewhere else.

Nothing is happening in my donkey.

I'm the one doing the cooking.

It goes in and it goes out, but nothing comes out.

I become both a giver and a taker of shit.

I wonder if there are many men in South Africa like me?

Ek is onsigbaar sonder whisky

Sy het die swaarheid van 'n baie ligte persoon gehad

Hy het die ligtheid van 'n baie swaar persoon gehad

Saam was hulle onbewus van swaartekrag

en ander oënskynlike natuurwette

Saam het hulle gesweef

I'm invisible without whisky

She had the heaviness of a very light person

He had the lightness of a very heavy person

Together they were oblivious of gravity

and other ostensible Laws of nature

Together they floated

www.ingramcontent.com/pod-product-compliance
Lightning Source LLC
Chambersburg PA
CBHW071404300426

44114CB00016B/2180